Central Eurasian water crisis

Note to the reader from the UNU

The key concepts of the United Nations University programme on Sustainable Resource Management are sustainable use of land and water resources, and the vulnerability of ecosystems to human-induced and natural environmental changes. The programme centres around a number of scientifically solid, field-based projects with closely interrelated objectives.

This book emanates from the research project entitled "Hydropolitics and Eco-political Decision-making." The project aims to identify the issues in disputes concerning trans-boundary water resources; selected alternative scenarios that could lead to the solution of complex problems related to water and environment; and recommended processes through which the concerned countries are likely to agree on mutually satisfactory solutions to the problems by sharing resources and benefits. The research project is also intended to provide a comprehensive and objective environmental management setting for the sustainable development of international water bodies. In its initial phase, the project focused on trans-boundary freshwater resources in the Middle East and Asia.

The United Nations University Press series on Water Resources Management and Policy publishes the results of the UNU and related research in response to the United Nations Agenda 21, Chapter 18 ("Protection of the Quality and Supply of Freshwater Resources: Application of Integrated Approaches to the Development, Management and Use of Water Resources").

Central Eurasian water crisis: Caspian, Aral, and Dead Seas

Edited by Iwao Kobori and
Michael H. Glantz

**United Nations
University Press**

TOKYO · NEW YORK · PARIS

United Nations University Press
The United Nations University, 53-70, Jingumae 5-chome,
Shibuya-ku, Tokyo 150, Japan
Tel: (03) 3499-2811   Fax: (03) 3406-7345
E-mail: mbox@hq.unu.edu

UNU Office in North America
2 United Nations Plaza, Room DC2-1462-70, New York, NY 10017
Tel: (212) 963-6387   Fax: (212) 371-9454   Telex: 422311 UN UI

United Nations University Press is the publishing division of the United Nations University.

Cover design by Joyce C. Weston

Printed in the United States of America

UNUP-925
ISBN 92-808-0925-3

Library of Congress Cataloging-in-Publication Data

   Central Eurasian water crisis: Caspian, Aral, and Dead seas/
edited by Iwao Kobori and Michael H. Glantz.
      p. cm.
Includes bibliographical references and index.
ISBN 9280809253 (pbk.)
1. Water-supply-Asia.   2. Sustainable development-Asia.
3. Water rights-Asia.   I. Kobori, Iwao, 1924– . II. Glantz,
Michael H.
TD299.C66   1998
333.91′0095—dc21   97-45286
CIP

Contents

Foreword

Bo Kjellén

The United Nations Conference on Environment and Development, held in Rio de Janeiro in 1992, created a new awareness of the fundamental problems of sustainable development. The Conference agreed on a broad programme of action leading into the twenty-first century – Agenda 21. Through the joint efforts of governments, non-governmental organizations, and the scientific community, we have all begun to realize that global environmental problems in the long term may threaten human survival. We need to tackle them urgently, and the responses have to be on a global scale – this is an essential challenge for the United Nations system in the decades to come.

Among these problems of global significance, the issue of the world's water resources warrants special attention. This was recognized by the main follow-up body to Rio, the Commission on Sustainable Development, which decided to carry out a comprehensive water assessment, to be considered by the UN General Assembly in 1997. Several agencies are involved in this work, and the Stockholm Environment Institute plays a key role. The international community needs to focus on water for political, economic, and social reasons. First of all, water is the strategic factor in ensuring long-term food security for the growing world population. My involvement in the work on the UN Convention to Combat Desertification, signed in 1994, has made me acutely aware of the fact that almost 1 billion of the world's population today live in drylands, in fragile ecosystems, sensitive to human activities and to the hazards of climatic factors. Second, experience has shown that there are essential elements of foreign policy and security policy linked to water. Some people maintain that water will become a more serious cause for conflict than oil in the future. Be that as it may, it is clear that shared water resources can lead to a downward spiral of conflict and war – but it is also obvious that the need for cooperation and perceived mutual interests can lead to an upward spiral of consultation and joint action.

For these varied reasons, I feel particularly honoured and pleased to preface this book. It sets a number of particularly important problems of inland seas with shared water resources in a broad perspective, presented by eminent scientists focused on the Aral Sea, the Caspian Sea, and the Dead Sea. I have myself had the opportunity to be involved in the efforts to face the situation in the Aral Sea basin, a problem of a man-made desert, which is clearly of global significance. The disappearing Aral Sea is a major environmental and human disaster to which nobody can remain indifferent. The specific studies on inland seas in this book will no doubt help all of us – and in particular the governments concerned – to find practical and practicable solutions that will really benefit the hard-hit people living in these regions.

But we also know that national and international action is difficult in a world with many pressures and conflicts of interest. This book gives us the opportunity to benefit from an expert overview of issues and possible solutions in some of the most serious problem regions of the world. We can compare, see similarities and differences, link political, economic, social, and technical factors, and improve understanding as a basis for action. Is is indeed an essential role for the United Nations University.

1

Perspectives on water environment management

Juha I. Uitto

Water is a finite natural resource, essential for the sustenance of life on earth. Agenda 21, a major outcome of the United Nations Conference on Environment and Development (UNCED), popularly referred to as the Earth Summit, held in Rio de Janeiro, Brazil, in June 1992, states that effectively integrated management of water resources is important to all socio-economic sectors relying on water. Rational allocation prevents conflict and enhances the social development of local communities, as well as economic planning and productivity.

Competition for fresh water resources, particularly in the arid and semi-arid regions of the world, is bound to lead to conflicts in the near future among countries sharing international freshwater bodies. Furthermore, environmental degradation resulting from intensive water development and usage, as well as from global change, plays an important role in the socio-economic and political processes both nationally and internationally.

Chapter 18 of Agenda 21 on the "Protection of the Quality and Supply of Freshwater Resources" further identifies the great importance of trans-boundary water resources and their use to the riparian states. It recognizes that cooperation among the riparian states is desirable in conformity with existing agreements and other relevant arrangements, taking into account the interests of all riparian states concerned.

Issues pertaining to the management of international waters for sustainable development figure prominently in the research programme of the United Nations University. Environment and sustainable development are one of the five main areas of concentration in the UNU programme. The programme entitled "Global Life-Support Systems" responds to Agenda 21. In 1993, the UNU appointed a high-level advisory team to explore ways by which the institution could contribute to the implementation of Agenda 21 and the Earth Charter. With a view to providing bases for sustainable environmental and political management of critical natural resources, the overall objectives of UNU activities in the field of the management of international waters focus on the comprehensive and objective study of regions in which countries share major international water bodies.

In 1993, the UNU organized a project focusing on the international waters of the Middle East, including the Nile, the Jordan, and the Euphrates–Tigris rivers. Water is seen as one of the major concerns in international politics in regions where fresh water is considered to be a scarce resource. The UNU Middle East Water Forum was organized, together with the International Water Resources Association and the United Nations Environment Programme (UNEP), in Cairo, Egypt, in February 1993. It brought together key actors from the countries in the region, many of whom had been involved in Middle East peace talks. The project looked at the international waters of the Middle East from the point of view of management for sustainable and peaceful purposes. It was, indeed, seen as making a contribution to the Middle East peace process by providing objective, scientifically based knowledge as well as management options for the utilization of regional trans-boundary water resources. Outputs of that Forum included the publication of three major books on water resources management and politics in the region (Biswas, 1994; Murakami, 1995; Wolf, 1995).

An ongoing activity that relates to environmental management focuses on the Aral Sea region, where a major environmental disaster, shared by a number of independent nations, has built up over a 30-year period. The Aral Sea is one of the regions assessed in the UNU project on "Critical Zones in Global Environmental Change" (Kasperson et al., 1995). In 1992, the UNU joined with the Global Infrastructure Fund Research Foundation of Japan to organize a symposium on the "Environmental Management of the Aral Sea

Region." A follow-up symposium, reporting on research progress, was held in December 1993 (Paoletto, 1992, 1994). The objective of these symposia was to seek solutions to the problems of the Aral Sea region through international cooperation.

The Asian Water Forum, organized in Bangkok in early 1995, focused on conflict resolution with regard to water allocations between the countries sharing three major Asian water bodies in Asia – the Mekong, the Ganges–Brahmaputra, and the Salween rivers. A related objective was to study issues related to industrial development, environment, and navigation along these rivers. Once again, the aim was to bring to the same table scholars and policy makers from the riparian countries, as well as representatives of major international organizations and donor agencies active in the regions of concern. Thus, these activities have major policy implications that go well beyond just academic research.

Building on past activities and common theoretical frameworks, the UNU cooperated with the International Lake Environment Committee Foundation and the UNEP International Environmental Technology Centre to organize a Forum focusing on water resources management in the major enclosed inland seas in the Central Eurasian region – the Aral Sea, the Caspian Sea, and the Dead Sea. This Forum was part of a three-day activity focused on the Central Eurasian water crises (27 December 1995 in Tokyo and 28–29 December 1995 in Otsu). With the invaluable cooperation of the Japan International Cooperation Agency, leading scholars were brought together from the countries in the region, including Kazakhstan, Uzbekistan, and Iran, as well as Russia, the United States, and Japan, who could speak on the common as well as unique problems facing the Caspian, Aral, and Dead Seas. The goal was to stimulate new, creative ideas for solving the environmental, social, economic, and political problems that are likely to emerge over shared water resources, especially inland seas. This volume is the outcome of that Forum.

References

Biswas, A. K. (ed.). 1994. *International Waters of the Middle East: From Euphrates-Tigris to Nile.* Bombay: Oxford University Press.

Kasperson, J. X., R. E. Kasperson, and B. L. Turner II. 1995. *Regions at Risk: Comparisons of Threatened Environments.* Tokyo: United Nations University Press.

Murakami, M. 1995. *Managing Water for Peace in the Middle East: Alternative Strategies.* Tokyo: United Nations University Press.

Paoletto, G. (ed.). 1992. *Environmental Management of the Aral Sea Region: Finding Solutions to One of the World's Major Environmental Disasters*. Report of the International Symposium held at UNU Headquarters Building, Tokyo, Japan, 29 September 1992. Tokyo: The United Nations University and Global Infrastructure Fund Research Foundation of Japan.

———— (ed.). 1994. *Report of the Seminar on the Aral Crisis: Second UNU/GIF Meeting on the Environmental Management of the Aral Sea Region*. Tokyo: The United Nations University and Global Infrastructure Fund Research Foundation of Japan.

Wolf, A. T. 1995. *Hydropolitics along the Jordan River: Scarce Water and Its Impact on the Arab–Israeli Conflict*. Tokyo: United Nations University Press.

Part I
Introduction

2

Central Eurasian water perspectives and arid land studies

Iwao Kobori

I participated in the Tokyo University Iraq–Iran Archeological Mission in 1956. Since then I have visited many rivers and lakes on the Eurasian landmass. Most of these are geographically located in arid and semi-arid areas where sparse precipitation and high evaporation rates are dominant. Among the world's inland lakes, the Dead Sea, the Caspian Sea, and the Aral Sea are of extraordinary interest from the point of view of arid land studies and for the need for future peaceful and sustainable economic development.

The water level of the Dead Sea, one of the deepest inland lakes and with the highest salinity levels, has dropped in recent years, while the water level of the Caspian Sea has risen. The Aral Sea is drying up, and its surface area has decreased by about half. Although we know these facts, there is not enough information for use in long-range planning. These regional changes are proceeding at different time and space scales and for different reasons. We must rescue and rehabilitate these lake regions if there is to be any hope for sustainable development in and around them in the not-too-distant future.

In the case of the Dead Sea, the problem for the future is how to stop the decrease in sealevel and how to revitalize the Dead Sea region. One solution might be to resort to dramatic mega-engineering efforts, another might to support steady, small-scale development along its coastline. Activities such as these will require careful management.

About 40 years ago, a colleague and I translated a book by Ivanov Omsky, in which there was a lot of praise for state plans concerning the transformation of the natural environment, especially in the arid areas of the Soviet Union. The miracle of the development of the Hungry Steppe near Tashkent (Uzbekistan) and the construction of the Karakum Canal (in Turkmenistan), which enabled large segments of the Karakum Desert to be irrigated and developed for agricultural production, have been well publicized. The development of the cotton culture industry in the Central Asian republics, such as Uzbekistan, has been very well known.

After I attended the Fifth All-Union Soviet Geographical Congress (1970, Leningrad) and the International Geographical Congress (1976, Moscow and Ashchabad), I received many papers on arid lands. However, up to the 1980s there was no mention of the Aral Sea crisis, especially the shrinking of the sea basin and its influence on the inhabitants.

I first visited the Dead Sea (Jordan) in 1956, and since then I have visited the upper branches of the Jordan River and its tributaries in Lebanon and Syria several times. In 1961, I visited the Dead Sea and the Jordan Valley on the Israeli side. Unfortunately, the water problems of that area have been largely a function of political tension between Israel and its neighbouring Arab countries. The construction of a national water pipeline by Israel has diminished the water flow from Lake Tiberias into the Jordan River; as a result, the sealevel of the Dead Sea has fallen. The inequitable distribution of water between Israel and the occupied territories has caused a high level of tension between the inhabitants of both regions.

Israel, the PLO, and Jordan agreed on a peace treaty in 1993, although it is a partial one. This was a milestone on the road to peace, even though many difficulties are likely to lie ahead. However, in reality, the planning of water resources is still under debate on both sides of the Jordan Valley and among outside authorities.

In 1958 I visited Professor Reifenberg, the author of *The Desert and the Sown*. He spoke of the Med–Dead Sea Canal Project. I met Eng. Batz, Vice-Mayor of Beer-Sheva, who was involved in the planning of the Second Suez Canal. During my interviews in 1961, I never expected the evolution of the Arab–Israeli conflicts that we now see. The time has come to reconsider the canal plan, but as yet no assessment has been made of this theoretical plan, and the consensus of relevant countries has not yet been forthcoming.

For the Caspian Sea, one of the largest lakes in the world, environmental studies suggest that the problem of sealevel change is not so acute in comparison with that of the Aral Sea. None the less, the recent increase in the level of the Caspian Sea, especially along the southern and south-western shorelines, pollution by petroleum industries, and the decline of lucrative fisheries will cause problems for the inhabitants of the Caspian Sea coastal region. The Caspian is now surrounded by five states: Iran, Azerbaijan, Russia, Kazakhstan, and Turkmenistan. Just a few years ago there were only two littoral states – the Soviet Union and Iran. In addition, each former Soviet Central Asian republic has its own national political and socio-economic problems, making it difficult to coordinate these states for the sake of resolving the Caspian Sea problems.

Since the disintegration of the Soviet Union, the Central Asian republics have suffered from severe economic crises, despite the re-emergence and importance of commerce and trade in traditional bazaars. The continued exploitation of hydrocarbon resources and the discovery of new ones may eventually serve to vitalize some of these economies. However, to benefit from the export of petrol or natural gas, close cooperation will be required with neighbouring countries, such as Iran and Turkey, as well as support from the world market-place. Under such conditions, Central Asian affairs cannot be viewed as isolated from happenings in other parts of the world.

Consider the role of Central Asia in history. The dry steppe of the Eurasian landmass has always been a crossroads of civilization, trade, commerce, and military conquests. Once flourishing political entities, such as Khorezm, declined after the destruction of their irrigation systems.

International cooperation for peaceful water management in critical areas

A new model of international cooperation is required for those critical areas in need of peaceful inter-state (i.e. trans-boundary) management of water resources. But who should be expected to take the initiative in this activity: international organizations, non-governmental organizations, national or local decision makers, the inhabitants, or some combination of them?

The environmental catastrophe in the Aral Sea basin has already received much attention from the international community. Turning interest and attention into concrete action, however, is no easy task. For example, the headquarters of Aral-related organizations have been busy receiving visitors who have come time and again to assess the crisis situation, but those visits have yielded very few results. The rehabilitation of the Aral Sea and its disaster zone needs very large investments. Given the increasing demands for scarce international funds, the international community must consider to what extent it should get involved. Good data about what is happening in the region require sustained monitoring of the physical aspects of ecological change, as well as the monitoring of socio-economic and cultural change.

As an ideal plan, the international community should consider establishing an international research centre in the region, whose first act should be to stop the exodus of able regional scientists to Moscow or abroad. Scholars outside the region often accept young researchers in their institutions and send bright students to the region. Japan, for example, has sent several missions either through government agencies or through non-governmental organizations, such as universities and the Global Infrastructure Fund.

Japan is very interested in Central Asia, and it now has a small reservoir of good researchers. Depending on those important human resources, Japan is very pleased to cooperate with international groups through the United Nations University (UNU), other international organizations, Japanese government authorities (such as the Japan International Cooperation Agency, the Environment Agency, or the Ministry of Education, Science and Culture), and other concerned ministries or foundations. The international community is now fostering cooperation through ongoing bilateral projects.

As regards the Caspian Sea, the present environmental situation, relatively speaking, does not appear to be acute. The rising sealevel is causing destruction in the low-lying coastal areas, but scientific analyses of the decadal-scale fluctuations of the Caspian Sea level do exist. For this reason, research on rivers flowing into the sea may be necessary. Because of the huge area of the sea and the resources in it, inter-state cooperation may be difficult. Attempts to establish regional cooperation are very recent. Under these conditions, a different approach from the case of the Aral Sea needs to be pursued.

Encouragement of cooperation among riparian countries and international groups involved in the region is very necessary. Cooperative efforts among riparian countries for ground and space surveys using advanced technology will be necessary. Furthermore, macro and micro socio-economic studies on the people in the Caspian Sea region should also be undertaken cooperatively. The exchange of researchers should be expanded and a fellowship for the region would be very welcome.

In the case of the Dead Sea basin, including the Jordan Valley, a multinational framework is already being developed. International organizations such as the United Nations and the European Union, and big powers such as the United States, Japan, and Canada, are keenly interested in the rehabilitation of this contested zone. The improvement of water works, especially for potable water for local inhabitants, is a high priority. Databases on the water resources are well developed. However, it is a very complicated process to coordinate planning in an area of scattered Palestinian territories, the occupied West Bank under Israeli control, and Israeli territory.

As an example, from a public health point of view, Gaza faces an inadequate water network (potable or seepage), because it is under heavy population pressure. A giant engineering scheme could improve the situation in the future, but urgent funding is needed now to address the acute problems that the local inhabitants face today. We cannot wait for a complete regional political settlement. Furthermore, addressing pressing water supply problems today could help the peace process. Better living conditions and improved infrastructure for inhabitants might accelerate a peaceful settlement of inter-state political tension in the region. Action in the future is very obvious: keep the peace permanently. It is time to keep alive and complete the peace process.

The second introductory chapter in this part is by Professor Kira, whose paper on world lakes and their problems provides a framework for the presentation of environmental problems facing inland bodies of water.

Part II on the Aral Sea contains a paper discussing creeping environmental problems in the context of the Aral Sea basin, an essay on the socio-economic development prospects of the region in the light of its Soviet history for most of the twentieth century, and a set of satellite images showing changes in the Aral Sea region over time. These papers are supplemented by three voices from the region. These brief papers were drawn from comments during the Forum discussion session.

Part III contains two essays, one from a Russian perspective and the other from an Iranian perspective, on environmental problems in the Caspian Sea region. The Caspian Sea level has risen considerably since 1977, creating havoc in riparian countries whose low-lying areas have been inundated by the relatively rapid increase in sealevel.

Part IV focuses on the Middle East and the Jordan River watershed. There is considerable concern that countries in the Middle East will eventually engage in conflict, not over ideological or religious issues but because of water shortages in the region. The two contributions in this section not only describe some of the regional problems related to water but propose political as well as engineering solutions.

The final chapter addresses the role of international organizations in assisting riparian countries in their attempts to devise ways of equitably and sustainably managing the water resources associated with inland drainage basins and the rivers that feed them.

3

Major environmental problems in world lakes

Tatsuo Kira

Everywhere in the world, lakes and reservoirs are becoming more and more important as the most dependable sources of water in large amounts. Lakes and reservoirs are more attractive water sources than rivers and underground water for big water consumers such as cities and industrial centres. In terms of size, number, and distribution, man-made lakes today are quite comparable with freshwater natural lakes.

On all the continents, however, the environments in those lakes and reservoirs are deteriorating rapidly and extensively due to various human impacts. Both the quantity and the quality of lakes' water resources are being threatened in that an increasing number of lakes have already lost not only their value as sources of water but also such traditional roles as the space for fisheries and waterborne transportation.

For this very reason, the International Lake Environment Committee (ILEC) was established soon after the First World Lake Conference held in Japan in 1984. Since 1986, ILEC has made efforts to formulate guiding principles and programmes on the environmentally sound management of lakes and their watersheds along the line of sustainable development policies. Its activities have so far included the publication of lake management guideline books (Jørgensen and Vollenweider, 1989; Jørgensen and Löffler, 1990; Hashimoto, 1991; Matsui, 1993; Jørgensen, 1993), convening training courses in lake management, symposia, and workshops, promoting environmental education in schools of several countries, supporting a series of World Lake Conferences, and, above all, compiling environmental data on world lakes. Detailed limnological and socio-economic data on some 220 lakes have already been accumulated and are being published by a joint project of ILEC, the United Nations Environment Programme (UNEP), and Lake Biwa Research Institute (LBRI and ILEC, 1988, 1989, 1990, 1991). Descriptive information on more than 500 lakes is also available for reference.

Figure 3.1 shows the range of water volume in relation to mean transparency for 145 lakes whose data had been published before 1990. The range covered is very wide, amounting to the order of 10^7, though most of the lakes are in a narrower range of 10^2–10^4 km^3. Transparency appears to depend on lake size, but certain lakes, e.g. shallow lakes on windy plains such as Lake Winnipeg (Canada) and Lake Balaton (Hungary), tend to have exceptionally small Secchi depth values.

A preliminary synthesis of the accumulated data on world lakes and reservoirs revealed the global prevalence of six types of environmental disruption as major problems of urgent concern (fig. 3.2): decline of water level, accelerated siltation, acidification, eutrophication, toxic contamination, and extermination of ecosystems and biota.

Declining water levels

Falling water levels and the resulting shrinkage of lake areas are due to the overuse of water drawn from the lake itself or from inflowing or outflowing rivers.

The extreme case of the Aral Sea is now widely known. Similar situations are also reported for other Central Asian lakes such as the Caspian Sea in the middle decades of the twentieth century (Golubev, 1992), Lake Balkhash in Kazakhstan, Lake Qinghai in China, and some lakes in Iran. Lake Mono in California also lost about 30 per cent of its former area owing to a fall in the water level of 11 m, and suffers from raised salt concentration in the lake water (as does the Aral Sea), owing to the diversion of 85 per cent of its tributary river water to the city of Los Angeles.

Aside from such lakes in the arid zone, the water level in other

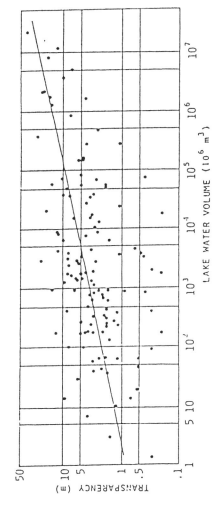

Fig. 3.1 **The transparency of lake water in relation to lake water volume in 145 lakes and reservoirs of the world**

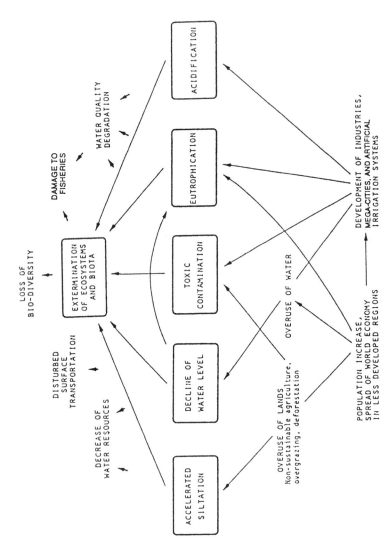

Fig. 3.2 **Six major environmental problems of world lakes and reservoirs**

16

lakes has often been significantly lowered by dredging their outlets in order to increase the capacity of hydroelectric power generation in outflowing rivers. This has often caused the temporary advance of eutrophication, as, for instance, was the case in Lake Sevan in Armenia (Oganesian, 1991).

Rapid siltation

Rapid siltation of lakes is the result of soil erosion accelerated by the overuse of farming and grazing lands, deforestation, the over-harvesting of fuelwood, and other imprudent land uses in lake catchment areas.

This is a very serious problem facing many lakes and reservoirs in China, India, Africa, and other less developed countries. Particularly alarming is the fact that cultivated fields and pastures, which have been sustainably used as more or less stationary semi-natural systems for centuries, are being devastated almost irreversibly by overuse. Overpopulation, as well as the residents' strong desire for more cash income to buy imported industrial products, has encouraged the abandonment of traditional sustainable methods of land use. The same situation is causing desertification in arid regions and forest destruction in the humid tropics.

The silt load of lake water, indicated by the concentration of suspended solids, is significantly correlated with the area of cultivated land per lake water volume in lakes in humid/subhumid climates, as illustrated in figure 3.3. A correlation in the arid zone could not be detected owing to the scarcity of available data.

Acidification

Acidification of lake water is caused by the input of acid air pollutants such as acid rain and dry fallout, either directly on the lake surface or indirectly via inflowing rivers.

Tens of thousands of small lakes in northern and central Europe and in North America have already become too acid to allow fish to breed there and, in extreme cases, almost any kinds of animals to survive. At present, the acidification of lake water is largely confined to rather limited regions such as Scandinavia, parts of central Europe, the north-eastern United States, and neighbouring parts of Canada, most probably owing to particular geological conditions, though acid precipitation itself occurs more widely over the northern hemisphere.

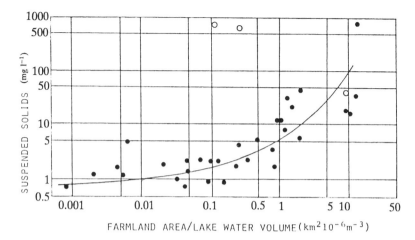

Fig. 3.3 **The relation between the concentration of suspended solids in lake water and the area of farmland in corresponding catchment areas (Note: closed and open circles refer, respectively, to lakes and reservoirs in humid/subhumid regions and those in arid regions)**

However, soil scientists have recently tried to predict how long it will take for the buffer capacity of the soil to be exhausted by continued acid precipitation. The predicted value of course depends on soil type, but may range, e.g. in Japanese soils, from several years to several decades. This is an alarming prediction, which suggests that the acidification of lake water may sooner or later become a global issue.

The progress of eutrophication

Eutrophication is spreading, owing to the combined effects of such factors as industrialization, the urban concentration of populations, changing ways of life toward mass consumption and mass dumping, the increased application of fertilizers on cropfields, deforestation and other types of ecosystem disturbance in catchment areas, the submergence of terrestrial biomass caused by reservoir construction, aquaculture within lakes, and so on.

Eutrophication has been, and perhaps will continue to be, the most widespread type of environmental pollution of water bodies. It is expanding rapidly from industrialized or urban areas to rural areas, from small streams to larger rivers, from small lakes to larger lakes, and from inland waters to coastal marine waters. The current situation in some lakes of overpopulated areas is critical, because newly growing large cities have to depend for their water supply on hypertrophic lake water filled with blooms of blue-green algae. Ecotechnological measures are not effective enough to overcome the crisis in the short term, and large-scale environmental technology such as sewage treatment systems is too expensive to be easily adopted.

Contamination with man-made toxics

The post-war epoch of environmental pollution started almost 40 years ago with a series of heavy metal contamination events in coastal and inland waters of Japan and some other countries. The situation has not yet been improved very much. The development of monitoring and warning systems for toxic contamination may prevent the recurrence of such tragedies as Minamata disease (caused by mercury poisoning) in industrialized countries, but many water bodies, including lakes and reservoirs, still remain dangerously contaminated. The kinds of identified toxins have significantly increased, including various kinds of mutagens and carcinogens whose risks have to be managed in a different way from those of heavy metals, agro-chemicals, etc.

There are also indications that contamination is spreading to less developed parts of the world, keeping pace with the advance of industrialization and urbanization. During ILEC's survey of world lake environments, however, it was recognized that information on toxic contamination of lakes in less developed countries, especially reliable numerical data, was disappointingly scarce. Here is one of the most urgent needs for international cooperation.

The collapse of aquatic ecosystems

The collapse of aquatic ecosystems and loss of biodiversity in natural lakes is the ultimate result of all the above-mentioned five processes.

Freshwater ecosystems are by no means as rich in plant and animal species as terrestrial ecosystems, but they are highly specialized with a high percentage of endemic species. For instance, the current number of fish species is said to amount to 22,000, of which one-third live in freshwater environments. In relation to the very limited area of inland waters, this percentage is surprisingly high and indicates the diversity of freshwater environments and the profound effect of geographical isolation.

Lake ecosystems, with their unique environment and biota, are very vulnerable to or intolerant of disturbance from outside. This is shown by the frequent invasion of alien species and their explosive prolification in many lakes. The opportunities for such immigration are ever increasing owing to the development of intercontinental travel and transportation. Waterweeds of New World origin are flourishing and suppressing native species in Old World lakes (e.g. *Elodea canadensis*, *E. nuttallii*, *Egeria densa*) and vice versa (e.g. *Myriophyllum spicatum*). It is said that Nile perch, a big carnivorous fish introduced into Lake Victoria, have already exterminated some 200 native fish species, a greater part of which are endemic to the lake (Chamberlain, 1993). The recent invasion by zebra mussel (*Dreissena polymorpha*) from Europe of the Great Lakes of North America offers another very remarkable example (Nalepa and Schlosser, 1993). Similar cases are known from many other lakes.

Lake ecosystems are also vulnerable to environmental changes. The excessive advance of such processes as siltation, water level decline (and resultant salinization), acidification, toxic contamination, and eutrophication may lead to the eradication of high plants and animals in the lake. We are thus losing highly characteristic gene pools in lake ecosystems from time to time.

The exploding world population and developing industries are always thirsty for fresh water. A critical shortage of freshwater resources may possibly arrive sooner than that of food in the near future. As this brief review shows, the critical situation of world lake environments should properly be placed among the important environmental problems of global scale because of its worldwide occurrence and profound influence on human life. In order to halt its further advance, concerted international efforts are indispensable. The International Lake Environment Committee sincerely hopes that the Fifth World Lake Conference (Stresa, 1993), together with the preceding and subsequent conferences, will take significant steps forward in responding to the challenge of this problem.

Acknowledgements

This paper originally appeared in *Memorie dell'Istituto Italiano di Idrobiologia*, 52: 1–7, 1993, and is reprinted with permission. The original text has been partially modified and/or abridged by the editors.

References

Chamberlain, J. 1993. "Lake Victoria: A tropical sea in distress." *Our Planet* 5(1), pp. 9–11.

Golubev, G. N. 1992. "Environmental problems of large Central Asian lakes." In: Proc. Symp., *Water Resources Management – With Views of Global and Regional Scales*. Otsu: UNEP and ILEC, pp. 55–63.

Hashimoto, M. (ed.). 1991. *Guidelines of Lake Management, Vol. 2, Socio-economic Aspects of Lake Reservoir Management*. Otsu: ILEC and UNEP.

Jørgensen, S. E. (ed.). 1993. *Guidelines of Lake Management, Vol. 5, Management of Lake Acidification*. Otsu: ILEC and UNEP.

Jørgensen, S. E. and H. Löffler (eds.). 1990. *Guidelines of Lake Management, Vol. 3, Lake Shore Management*. Otsu: ILEC and UNEP.

Jørgensen, S. E. and R. A. Vollenweider (eds.). 1989. *Guidelines of Lake Management, Vol. 1, Principles of Lake Management*. Otsu: ILEC and UNEP.

LBRI (Lake Biwa Research Institute) and ILEC (International Lake Environment Committee) (eds.). 1988–1991. *Data Book of World Lake Environments: A Survey of the State of World Lakes*, 4 vols. Otsu: ILEC and UNEP.

Matsui, S. (ed.). 1993. *Guidelines of Lake Management, Vol. 4, Toxic Substances Management in Lakes and Reservoirs*. Otsu: ILEC and UNEP.

Nalepa, T. F. and D. W. Schlosser (eds.). 1993. *Zebra Mussels – Biology, Impacts and Control*. Boca Raton, FL.: Lewis Publishers.

Oganesian, R. O. 1991. "Anthropogenic eutrophication of Lake Sevan and ways of preventing its negative consequences." Lecture at Lake Biwa Research Institute.

Part II
The Aral Sea

4

Creeping environmental problems in the Aral Sea basin

Michael H. Glantz

Introduction

With Mikhail Gorbachev's policy of *glasnost* (openness) in the mid-1980s, the international community received confirmation of what it had been able to detect from space at least since the mid-1970s – the gradual decline of the Aral Sea. Since the early 1960s, when the leaders of the Soviet Union embarked on a programme to increase river diversions in order to expand irrigated cotton production in this arid region, the sealevel has declined about 15 metres or so and its surface area has been reduced by half. Primary attention of policy makers and, later, multilateral development banks and environmental groups was focused on the declining Aral Sea level. This was *the* most visible impact from space and on the ground of reduced flow of the sea's two major feeder rivers, the Amudarya and the Syrdarya.

Although the decline in the level of the Aral Sea was the most obvious environmental change in the basin, there were several other adverse environmental changes as well. Because of the "creeping" nature of these environment-related changes (pollution of river and sea water, air quality degradation, deterioration of human health, desertification, and so forth), decision makers have had difficulty in addressing ways to slow down, arrest, or reverse the gradually occurring adverse changes. Perhaps the notion of creeping environmental problems (of which sealevel change is but one) can serve as an "umbrella" notion to encompass several of the environmental changes occurring in the Aral Sea basin. Eventually, however, these incremental changes have increasingly been perceived by some observers as having accumulated to such an extent as to have turned into crises. If Central Asian republics in the Aral basin can be convinced to address slow-onset, low-grade, long-term, cumulative environmental changes cooperatively and in a timely way, the adverse consequences could be mitigated and, perhaps, even averted.

The shrinking of the Aral Sea in Central Asia has captured the attention and interest of governments, environment and development organizations, the lay public, and the media around the globe (e.g. Orechkine, 1990; Ellis, 1990; *The Economist*, 1991, 1994; O'Dy, 1991; UNU, 1992). Considered a quiet catastrophe, referred to in the former Soviet Union as a "Quiet Chernobyl" (e.g. Glantz and Zonn, 1991), one that has evolved slowly, almost imperceptibly, over the past few decades, the demise of the Aral Sea has become acknowledged as one of the major human-induced environmental degradations of the twentieth century. The Aral basin was singled out by the International Geographical Union (IGU) in the early 1990s as one of the Earth's critical zones (see Kasperson et al., 1995).

Whereas societies respond (i.e. react) relatively quickly to step-like adverse environmental changes or to problems perceived by experts or elements of the public as crises, for example "rapid-onset hazards" (Palm, 1990), they have much more difficulty in developing awareness of the risks associated with slow-onset, low-grade change. This paper is as much about the nature of creeping environmental problems as it is about environmental change in the Aral Sea basin. It attempts to draw attention to the general *notion* of creeping environmental problems (CEPs) and societal responses to them, to develop a framework for characterizing CEPs in general, and to suggest the utility of applying that notion to recent environmental changes in the Aral Sea basin. The overriding objective of this chapter is not to provide the reader with a detailed assessment of creeping changes in the Aral Sea basin (for this assessment, see Glantz, 1998), but to spark discussion of ways to identify and overcome constraints on societal responses to creeping environmental change.

Introduction to the notion of creeping environmental problems

We are constantly bombarded in our daily lives with bad news about the environment. Some of that news is about environmental problems of a global nature and some of it is about problems at the local level. Some of these problems have long lead-times before their adverse consequences become apparent, whereas others develop over relatively shorter time-frames. The list of these environment-related problems is quite long and is still growing: air pollution, acid rain, global warming, ozone depletion, deforestation, desertification, droughts, famines, and the accumulation of nuclear and solid waste are the results of long-term, low-grade, and slow-onset cumulative processes. These kinds of problems can be called creeping environmental problems (CEPs), as opposed to rapid-onset natural hazards, such as earthquakes, hurricanes, tornadoes, tsunamis, storm surges, riverine floods, and severe winter storms. The schematic diagrams in figures 4.1 and 4.2 illustrate some of the differences between these two types of environmental changes. Creeping environmental problems cut across academic disciplines, political ideologies, continents, and cultures.

A major feature that CEPs share is that a change in a creeping environmental problem does not make it much worse today than it was yesterday; nor is the rate or degree of change tomorrow likely to be much different from that of today. So societies (individuals as well as government bureaucrats) do not, for the most part, recognize changes severe enough to cause them to treat their environments any differently than they had on previous days. Yet incremental changes in environmental conditions accumulate over time with the eventual

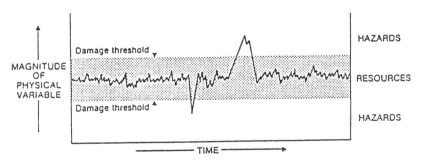

Fig. 4.1 **Schematic of a rapid-onset natural hazard (Source: Burton and Hewett, 1974)**

27

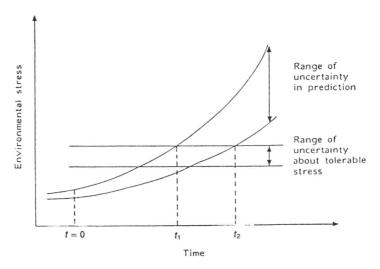

Fig. 4.2 **Schematic of slow-onset (creeping) environmental problems (Source: Döös, 1994)**

result that, after some perceived if not objectively defined threshold of change has been crossed, those unimportant imperceptible increments of change "suddenly" appear as major degradation. If no action is then taken, as is often the case, those incremental changes will likely continue to mount until a full-blown crisis emerges.

Many changes to the environment are not considered detrimental in their early stages and, if arrested early enough in the process, would not appear at all on anyone's list of environmental problems. Such changes would likely be viewed as environmental transformation and not as degradation. For example, the cutting down of a small part of a mangrove forest to create a shrimp pond would not necessarily signal a stage in the destruction of a mangrove forest ecosystem (transformation). If, however, numerous ponds were to be constructed in the same location, then the mangrove forest ecosystem and its interactions with other ecosystems would eventually cease (degradation).

Thresholds

At a workshop on "Adaptive Ecological Characterization," sociologist John Petterson (1995) noted the importance of thresholds in environmental change.

Ecosystems, regardless of how they are defined, must be viewed in the context of *accelerated* change in the dominant variable, i.e., the social, political, economic, technological, and other factors that have altered the larger environmental context of every ecosystem or subsystem. [Societal] change is not occurring in a linear fashion and, therefore, concern should be on *thresholds* at which irreversible consequences are initiated.

For each of the creeping environmental changes there may be identifiable thresholds beyond which continued degradation of the environment will increase the likelihood of irreversible changes in a societally favoured ecosystem. Thresholds, however, are easier to talk about than to detect. In fact, in many cases they may be identifiable only in retrospect, after they have been surpassed.

When discussing thresholds of awareness of environmental change, it is necessary to consider *whose* awareness we are concerned with. Levels of awareness of changes in the environment will increase as the environmental change persists and worsens. At first, for such CEPs as deforestation and desertification, changes may be noted by individuals at the local level but may not be seen as a threat of any sort and may go unreported to local or regional authorities or to national researchers. For truly global issues such as global warming or stratospheric ozone depletion, it would likely be a scientific researcher who first noticed an incremental environmental change.

As the environmental change is believed to have intensified in time (i.e. taken on a faster rate), in space (i.e. affecting a larger surface area than expected), or in impact (i.e. adversely impinging on human activities), it may be brought to the attention of authorities by local officials and environmental researchers. At this level, such changes might capture the attention and interest of the media. A further deepening of the adverse consequences associated with the change could prompt awareness at the national policy-making level, as well as of the international media, which can internationalize awareness of what had originally been viewed as a local environmental problem. Who it is that first generates awareness of a creeping environmental change and of subsequent thresholds of awareness can vary from one region to the next and from one type of creeping environmental change to another: it could be a farmer, a scientist, a policy maker, a news reporter.

There are several subjectively based thresholds that could be identified for creeping environmental problems: a first threshold relates to awareness of an environmental change that has not yet been considered a problem; a second threshold relates to awareness that a previously undetected environmental change has become a problem; a third threshold relates to the realization that the problem has reached a crisis stage; and a fourth one relates to a threshold that leads to concerted action to cope with the problem. With regard to the CO_2 issue, the scientific community has chosen a doubling of atmospheric CO_2 levels of the pre-industrial era (about AD 1750) as an arbitrary indicator of a threshold. A doubling, however, is of no particular scientific significance. No major changes in the atmosphere are expected to occur once that level of atmospheric CO_2 has been reached. Thus, it is a quantitative threshold that has been arbitrarily designated. Because these problems derive from slow-onset, low-grade, long-term, and cumulative environmental changes, it is not easy to identify universally accepted objective quantitative indicators of thresholds.

Steps of awareness

Threshold 1: Awareness of change
Agricultural people are busy with their daily routines and in most parts of the world that translates to human activities directly related to food production. Preoccupied with day-to-day efforts to eke out a living from the land, these people are likely to notice small changes in their environment. Those small changes are not considered to be an immediate problem, or perhaps even a problem at all. They are viewed as a modification or transformation of nature. In fact, such changes might at first be viewed as a precondition in the drive toward an improved quality of life for local inhabitants. Short-term benefits seem to override any concern about potential long-term implications of such small, seemingly benign, environmental changes. The rates of such change are not seen by anyone as threatening to human activities or to the long-term productivity of the environment. They may also be viewed as easily reversible.

Threshold 2: Awareness of a CEP
The recognition by an individual or a group that an environmental change has become a problem suggests that another threshold has been crossed. Not all observers will likely agree that a problem has emerged. Case histories of other CEPs, such as global warming and stratospheric ozone depletion, underscore that scientific uncertainties that surround an issue can be highlighted in such a way as to raise

questions about whether the environment has changed significantly and, if so, whether that change had become a societal problem requiring action. This raises issues of risk acceptance, risk avoidance, and risk-making, with different elements in a society exhibiting one of these predispositions toward risk. The existence of opposing views notwithstanding, a threshold of awareness has been crossed that prompts the attention of decision makers at the regional or national levels of government.

Threshold 3: Crisis awareness

Usually, a "whistle blower" or a champion to lead the call for combating the CEP emerges when that problem reaches a crisis level. A crisis can be defined as a crossroad or critical turning point. It has also been defined as a critical decision point (e.g. short time to act, high threat, high cost of inaction).

In the risk assessment literature related to environmental issues (e.g. Kahneman et al., 1982), the notion of "dread risk" or "dread factor" has been used. A dread factor refers to a more ominous situation than crisis, in that it relates to a situation with a perceived lack of control, or with imminent catastrophic potential, or with fatal consequences. Crisis does not equate to dread. Resorting to the citing of a dread risk is a tactic that can backfire if the alleged dread status of the CEP is shown to be unsupported by facts. In generating societal belief that a critical threshold has been crossed and that a CEP demands immediate attention, the media (national and international) are often instrumental.

Threshold 4: Awareness of the need to act

Awareness of a crisis, however, often fails to translate directly into societal responses. By now the local community has likely become overwhelmed by the CEP and its local impacts. Only the national or international community can help them to cope with the CEP. However, as is often the case, given the degree of scientific and economic controversy (i.e. uncertainties) that usually surrounds CEPs, policy makers can choose to delay the enactment of coping policy responses. Thus, the last of the thresholds focuses on action, taken domestically or internationally.

Threshold 5: Action

What does it mean to "take action" on a creeping environmental problem? Although there is a wide range of possible actions that could be taken in the name of seeking to resolve a CEP, meaningful actions can be identified in objective terms for each CEP. Those actions would need to be defined in terms of the goals to be achieved by particular actions: slow down the rate of a creeping environmental change; arrest the progression of the change; reverse the direction of the change; restore the ecosystem. Actions taken at the lowest level of effectiveness (i.e. slow down the rate of the adverse change) can be challenged as ineffective by those who want to confront the problem more aggressively. Thus, responses to questions such as "have policy makers taken action" to combat desertification or deforestation or global warming will not necessarily be in agreement, because varying levels of actions in response to a CEP could be taken.

In sum, we need to identify thresholds and to recognize that they would likely vary from one region to another, even for the same type of environmental degradation. What is that threshold of awareness and of crisis? When is the appropriate time to act on a creeping environmental change (Glantz, 1994)? Before applying the notion of CEP to the Aral Sea basin, a close scrutiny of a variety of known CEPs could be instructive in identifying objective ways to recognize thresholds before they appear.

Characteristics of CEPs

Several general characteristics can be used to categorize CEPs into subgroups: time and space scales, rates of change, levels of scientific uncertainty, levels of visible degradation, the seemingly impersonal nature of the causes of CEPs or their effects (e.g. the tragedy of the commons), degree of politicization of an issue, reversibility of the CEP, etc.

The perceived rate at which an environmental change takes place is very important when it comes to the timing of societal responses to those changes. Although there may be ways to identify those rates quantitatively, it is often the perception of those rates that prompts action. To policy makers, as well as to the general public, rates of change are often as important, if not more so, than the magnitude of the change. Slow rates of change do not provoke societal concern, let alone response. Rapid rates tend to lead to rapid responses by decision makers. Yet rates of environmental change are often quite controversial. The scientific and popular literature on each CEP yields a broad range of rates with little agreement among them. For example, for desertification in the West African Sahel, rates of desertification vary by an order of magnitude; even the sign of the change has fallen into question (Tucker et al., 1991). For tropical deforestation in the Brazilian Amazon, the variance is considerable, by a factor of seven (Parisi and Glantz, 1992). Interestingly, in the Brazilian case, that rate of change varied from one year to the next in the 1980s. Determining when specific CEP thresholds have been crossed is not an easy task.

The time-frame over which an environmental change develops into a full-blown environmental crisis affects the lead-time available for response by decision makers to any one of the various thresholds. Thus, perceptions about the need to respond to crisis situations can develop over long as well as short time-scales. Global warming and stratospheric ozone depletion are considered global changes that occur on a decades-to-centuries time-scale; deforestation, desertification, and inland sealevel changes are regional changes occurring from years to decades; droughts (and famines) are local- to regional-scale processes that develop over a period of several months to a few years.

It may seem odd to speak of, and lump together under the same "umbrella," creeping environmental problems that occur on various time-scales. One might ask, for example, if those concerned about famine avoidance can respond to that CEP in a matter of several months, why can't other decision makers respond to their CEP relatively quickly as well? To address this point, one needs to take into account the scope of the problem (its magnitude, intensity, duration, reversibility). Although scientists and policy makers may not know exactly when thresholds of environmental change will occur with regard to their CEP, they apparently believe they have enough lead-time to act, once the environmental change appears to have become a crisis.

Generally speaking, scientific uncertainties will always surround CEPs. For example, in the 1970s, researchers drew attention to spreading deserts in the West African Sahel, using photographs and satellite imagery to support their views. However, some scientists have suggested that the total area affected by desertification around the world had actually decreased by the end of the 1980s (Tucker et al., 1991). Even with regard to ozone depletion, an issue on which most scientists agree, a small but vocal backlash group has continued to challenge the evidence of ozone depletion in Antarctica.

For most CEPs there is a minority voice, often loud, that focuses on scientific uncertainties, as opposed to emphasizing what is known.

Such conflicting interactions among groups within the scientific community tend to weaken the resolve of non-scientists who are expected to act (the public, policy makers, the media). Given the state of scientific knowledge on most CEPs, one can likely find within the body of scientific literature viewpoints and quantitative information to support (or attack) any desired policy action. The selective use of information drawn from the scientific literature enables policy makers to pursue any decisions they wish, regardless of the reliability of the particular pieces of scientific information they choose to use. There is a need to collect and assess the wide range of rates in the scientific literature and in the popular media for each of the different CEPs, and to identify confidence limits for each of the plausible estimates (e.g. Parisi and Glantz, 1992).

Why do CEPs continue?

Creeping environmental problems change the environment in a negative, cumulative, and, at least for some period of time, invisible way. As a result of these minor insults to the environment over time, during which no obvious step-like changes occur, both governments and individuals tend to continue to view their "usual activities" as acceptable. They assume that their activities have little, if any, lasting impact on the environment. For many people, changing routine behaviour is not easy. As Eric Hoffer (1952, p. 3) suggested in his book *The Ordeal of Change*, "It is my impression that no one really likes the new. We are afraid of it. It is not only as Dostoyevsky put it that 'taking a new step, uttering a new word is what people fear most.' Even in slight things, the experience of the new is rarely without some stirring of foreboding." People fear change and, unless a crisis situation is perceived, they are not likely to behave differently in the absence of any incentive to do so.

Reasons (or excuses) for not taking action are many. For the global warming issue, one excuse for delaying a societal response has been its time-scale. If the doubling of carbon dioxide in the atmosphere is not expected to occur at least until the middle of the twenty-first century or later, why worry now? Why sacrifice (some would argue, squander) the scarce time (of politicians) and money (of societies) on such a distant problem? Yet, similar requests to delay responses also occur when confronted by creeping phenomena of much shorter time-scales, such as drought-related famines, sealevel decline, or degradation of urban water quality. Thus, creeping environmental problems can be defined in such a way that they can occur on several time-scales. The time factor becomes an important characteristic of a CEP, when the rate at which the CEP progresses is compared with the timing of the appearance of its adverse consequences.

Another reason fostering inaction on CEPs relates to scientific uncertainty. For example, why act at all regarding the global warming issue, when the scientific information about this particular CEP is sometimes contradictory and the remaining uncertainties are many? Yet, as suggested earlier, most environmental changes will likely be surrounded by scientific uncertainties. Nevertheless, policy makers are constantly forced to make policy decisions surrounded by uncertainty. Thus, whenever scientific uncertainty is used as an excuse for avoiding risks associated with decision-making, it should be challenged as a reason for delaying action.

Considerable discussion exists in the literature and the popular media about risk takers and those who are risk averse. The former are gamblers, whereas the latter tend to be more conservative in their approaches (and responses) to environmental change. Another related risk category that can be distinguished from these two existing ones is that of risk makers. These are decision makers whose decisions make risks for others but not necessarily for themselves. For example, reluctance to take action to slow down or stop desertification processes threatening a village far from the capital city where politicians live will likely have little political effect on decision makers at the national level. Their inaction generates growing risks for the distant inhabitants of a threatened village, but not necessarily for themselves. With regard to the declining Aral Sea level, in reality there were no adverse impacts on those in Moscow who made decisions that led to a declining Aral Sea level.

Most environmental problems do not affect an entire population of a country in a direct and visible way. At first, only those directly affected become concerned about local degradation. A central authority is likely to view that degradation as a local problem, even though similar processes may be occurring in other parts of the country (e.g. "we don't care if the Aral Sea disappears," "we don't care if species in the tropical rainforest disappear"). How, then, might the interest of central authorities (or unaffected citizens) in a local or regional creeping environmental problem be developed and sustained? The bottom line is that risk makers are often not held accountable for the environmental crises that result from their decisions.

Yet another constraint on timely action to address a CEP involves the fact that what appears to be an environmental crisis to one person may be viewed as an opportunity to someone else. For example, whereas some people may be concerned about environmental degradation, others might believe such degradation is the necessary result of a trade-off for economic development. Once past a crisis (i.e. defined as a crossroad or turning point), however, there may be a dread factor, an apocalyptic point beyond crisis from which there is no return to sustainability for the environment or the society dependent on it. With regard to the global warming issue, there have been several attempts by scientists to identify dread factors in order to provoke meaningful action from policy makers to combat it. With regard to any particular environmental problem, one can usually find examples of the use of dread factors to prompt political and societal action. The global warming situation provides a useful example of this.

In the mid-1970s modelling experiments proposed the use of $4 \times CO_2$ (4 times pre-industrial levels of carbon dioxide) as well as $2 \times CO_2$ experiments. The $4\times$ scenarios, however, were highly unrealistic and were dropped. A *doubling* of pre-industrial levels of CO_2 then took on the aura of a dread factor, although there was really nothing significant about using a doubling as a threshold of change. In the late 1970s, some scientists raised concern about the possibility of a breakup of the West Antarctic ice sheet, globally raising the sealevel rapidly by 8 metres or so. Further scientific research sharply reduced the probability of such an event. Yet another attempt to identify a dread factor was mention of the possibility of abrupt, highly disruptive changes in ocean currents over a period of a few decades (as opposed to centuries or millennia) in response to a warmer atmosphere (Broecker, 1987).

The search for an uncontestable crisis, if not dread risk, in the global warming issue continues, because previous dread factors have not captured the sustained concern of the public or of politicians. The lack of a dread risk notwithstanding, governments, for a variety of reasons, slowly began to cooperate on this CEP through the activities of the Intergovernmental Panel on Climate Change (IPCC) and the Intergovernmental Negotiating Committee (INC) for a Framework Convention on Climate Change. The UN Climate Convention was ratified on 21 March 1994 and, a year later, the first international Conference of the Parties was convened in Berlin, Germany, to discuss its implementation.

Döös (1994), using greenhouse gas emissions as an example, has suggested some reasons why actions by society to protect the environment have been slow and insufficient. He focused on the availability of objective scientific information: the reluctance of scientists to downplay scientific uncertainty, the focus by the media on sensational news rather than on scientific facts, deliberate neglect of scientific information for political and other reasons.

Jamieson (1991) identified and briefly summarized several reasons that affect timely policy response to climate change, which is a creeping environmental problem. Replacing the phrase "climate change" with CEP provides us with another set of factors that tend to delay societal responses to this type of environmental problem. Some of these are as follows:

1. The audience for [CEP] information is extremely diverse and the same message can mean different things to different people.
2. Many people ... are not scientifically equipped to understand more than the rudiments of a [CEP] issue.
3. The impacts of a [CEP] are perhaps more correctly represented probabilistically.... In general, people are notoriously bad at assimilating and reasoning about probabalistic information.
4. Significant [CEP] is a long-term, rather than a near-term, possibility. Most people, including most policymakers, are not used to thinking about such long-term events.
5. Many of the [CEP] effects on human welfare will be relatively invisible.... People have difficulty linking ... indirect impacts to an initial cause.
6. The onset of a [CEP] is gradual and uncertain, rather than dramatic and obvious.

Jamieson concluded that "our political and institutional structures are unlikely to respond aggressively enough to be helpful in the near term. So, for the present, the resource managers will be left to their own devices. The de facto policy is likely to be one of incrementalism or 'muddling through'" (Jamieson, 1991, p. 327).

The possibility also exists that, for issues as insidious as global warming, changes in climate at a regional or local level might not provide enough proof (e.g. *the* fingerprint) of a global climate change, because some CEPs may not exhibit a readily identifiable threshold of change. US Vice President Gore has often suggested that "[w]e are not unlike the laboratory frog that, when dropped into a pot of boiling water, quickly jumps out. But when placed in lukewarm water that is slowly heated, the frog will remain there until it is rescued" (Gore, 1992, p. 42).

The following section is an attempt to identify a set of environmental changes in the Aral Sea basin that can be viewed as creeping environmental problems. It provides a brief description of each CEP and issues a call for an intensive research effort to fill in a CEP matrix for each, identifying as best as possible thresholds of awareness alluded to earlier in the chapter. The region provides, in essence, a living laboratory for geographers, biologists, political scientists, water resource specialists, environmental philosophers, politicians, among others, where they can see, within the course of one generation, the impacts of economic decisions that were devoid of societal or environmental considerations.

CEPs and the Aral region

In the late 1950s, the Aral Sea was the Earth's fourth-largest inland body of water with respect to surface area. In 1960 the mean level of the Aral Sea was measured at 53.4 metres, its surface area at 66,000 km², and its volume at about 1,090 km³. A flourishing sea fishery industry existed, based on the exploitation of a variety of commercially valued species. During the past three decades, the Aral Sea region (see fig. 4.3) has become a major world-class ecological and socio-economic problem. It is now the sixth-largest inland water body.

The streamflows of the two perennial river systems, the Amudarya and Syrdarya, have, in the relatively recent past, sustained a stable Aral Sea level. Over the centuries, about half of the flow of the two rivers reached the Aral; a major expansion of irrigated cotton production altered this ecological balance. A sizeable portion of Central Asia's agricultural production is dependent on irrigation. Irrigated agriculture in the region pre-dates by millennia the era of tsarist conquests of the eighteenth and nineteenth centuries. What is "new" about irrigation in the region, however, is the huge amount of water diverted from the region's major rivers and, in turn, the large proportion of arable land devoted to cotton production. Beginning in the late 1970s, no water from the Syrdarya reached the Aral Sea, and the Amudarya supplied only a minimal and ever-decreasing volume. Large diversions, poor irrigation construction and maintenance, and mismanagement of water resources have been identified as major causes of the decreased flow to the Aral Sea (e.g. Bedford, 1996).

Awareness of the potential degradation surrounding the Aral Sea draw-down was widespread, even in the 1950s and 1960s, a time when

Fig. 4.3 **The Aral Sea region**

policy makers had a blind faith in the use of technological fixes to overcome obstacles in the paths to economic development and when the Soviet government did not allow organized dissent. The fate of the Aral Sea, under conditions of increasing diversions from the two major sources of Aral Sea water, was more or less known in the absence of any intervention to stop or limit the diversions. Articles about the risks of degradation appeared in Soviet journals, at least from the 1960s, and were translated into other languages. However, even the most ardent advocates of preserving the Aral under-estimated the range, rate of change, and intensity of the degradation that subsequently transpired.

There have been, and continue to be, decision makers who feel that the Aral Sea is of little intrinsic value to society. Thus, regardless of paying verbal homage to saving it, they do not care about its ulti-mate demise. Yet another group of people have supported the diversion of river water from the Amudarya and Syrdarya, knowing that such diversions were drawing down the level of the Sea. How-

39

ever, they had been led to believe that the Siberian rivers diversion project would eventually be approved, bringing water to Central Asia and possibly to the Aral Sea. Central Asians continue to believe that Russia's Siberian river water is owed to them by Russian leaders, because of their sacrifices to the Soviet Union in previous decades at the behest of the Soviet government to foster the all-out production of cotton for Russian textile factories. In fact, attempts are under way today to revive these diversion schemes, as well as to propose newer ones.

Thus, much is already known about the decline in the level of the Aral Sea: when it began, why it happened, who benefited and who suffered as a result of the decline, what actions were proposed to deal with the declining levels and with the deteriorating circum-Aral human health and environmental conditions, and so forth.

Although all this is known with some degree of certainty, it is important to note that this particular environmental change (slow-onset, low-grade, long-term, and cumulative decline in the level of the Aral Sea) is but one of a large family of such changes taking place in the Aral Sea basin. Although the primary focus of attention has been on the declining level of the Sea, in part because that change is highly visible (especially from space), it is but one creeping change in the basin to occur during the past half-century.

Creeping environmental problems in the Aral basin include the decline of the level of the Sea, reduced inflow to the Sea from the Amudarya and Syrdarya, monocropping, declining water quality, and adverse health effects. Because of the low-grade but cumulative nature of these problems, high-level policy makers, as well as low-level decision makers, have apparently had difficulties in identifying them as problems and then, once identified as such, in coping with them. As with other CEPs elsewhere, it is often difficult to identify thresholds of change that could serve to catalyse action to arrest environmental degradation. Water quality degrades slowly over time. Vegetative cover and human health also degrade slowly over time. As for streamflow, there were readily identifiable thresholds at which point all could see that a major change in the Aral Sea was near: for example, in the late 1970s when the Syrdarya's waters failed to reach the Sea. And, for a few years in the 1980s, the mighty Amudarya's water also failed to reach the Sea for the first time in recent history.

As a result of the lack of understanding of how societies can or should address such insidious environmental changes, there has been a tendency in the Aral Sea basin to "muddle through" with respect to the decision-making process. Only when a crisis has been perceived by a policy-making body has action been taken, usually in the form of a costly and rapid mobilization of human and financial resources. Such actions usually address the symptoms of the problem and not its root causes. As noted earlier, although the "muddling through/crisis response" paradigm *may* work in the richer industrialized countries, the value of the paradigm is much more questionable in countries with scarce resources such as those in Central Asia. Because they lack the resources needed to respond at all to such crises, they are forced to seek, if not rely on, assistance from donor countries and organizations. If such assistance is not forthcoming, the downward spiral of degradation continues.

Examples of CEP in the Aral Sea basin

The following brief examples of CEP are drawn from the Aral basin. They are meant to be suggestive, not to be an exhaustive list of creeping environmental changes in this Central Asian basin. With *glasnost* in the mid-1980s and the breakup of the Soviet Union in December 1991, interest in the region has grown sharply, in part for environmental reasons, but more so for geopolitical reasons (e.g. Glantz et al., 1993; Rashid, 1994; Eickelman, 1993).

Expansion of cotton acreage
The desire to expand cotton production onto desert land increased the dependence of Central Asian republics on irrigation and mono-cropping. Monocropping has adverse impacts on soil conditions, which prompts increasing dependence on mechanization, pesticides, herbicides, and fertilizers. Socio-economically, this is also risky in the sense that a regional economy based on a single crop is highly vulnerable to the variability of climate (especially climatic extremes) as well as to the whims of the market-place.

The demands of cotton production for irrigation water are high, at one time consuming over 50 per cent of agricultural water use in the region. Increased demands were met by increasing diversions from the Amudarya and the Syrdarya (fig. 4.4). Tables 4.1 and 4.2 show, respectively, the land under irrigation in three republics between 1950 and 1986, and the expansion of cotton acreage in Central Asia between 1940 and 1986. The data provided in these tables cover the post–World War II period of expansion of irrigation up to 1986, the year that the Aral crisis was first exposed to the world. Each

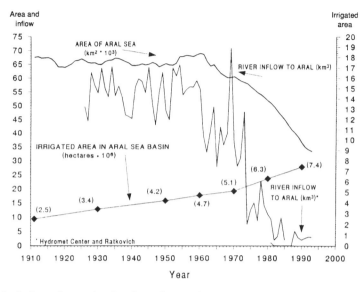

Fig. 4.4 **Irrigated area in the Aral Sea basin, 1910–1990, and river inflow to the Aral Sea and surface area of the Aral Sea, 1910–1993 (Source: Micklin and Williams, 1996)**

Table 4.1 **Land under irrigation, 1950–1986 (thousand hectares)**

Country	1950	1960	1965	1970	1975	1980	1985	1986
Uzbekistan	2,276	2,571	2,639	2,697	3,006	3,476	3,930	4,020
Tajikistan	361	427	468	518	567	617	653	662
Turkmenistan	454	496	514	643	819	927	1,107	1,185

Source: Critchlow (1991, p. 63).

year additional amounts of water were required for the new fields and for the flushing of salts from the old ones, suffering from increasingly salinized soils. In addition, starting in 1954 with the construction of the Karakum Canal in Turkmenistan, large amounts of water were diverted from the Amudarya to irrigate fields in that republic. The current estimate of withdrawals for the Karakum Canal from the Amudarya is about 15–20 km³ per year (or 23–30 per cent of flow).

The pie chart in figure 4.5 depicts the changes, since 1986, in the proportion of land (and therefore water for irrigation) devoted to

Table 4.2 **Cotton sowings, 1940–1986 (million hectares)**

Country	1940	1971–75[a]	1976–80[a]	1981–85[a]	1985	1986	Increase, 1940–1986 (%)
Uzbekistan	0.924	1.718	1.823	1.932	1.993	2.053	122
Tajikistan	0.106	0.264	0.295	0.308	0.312	0.314	196
Turkmenistan	0.151	0.438	0.504	0.534	0.560	0.650	330

Source: Critchlow (1991, p. 64).
a. Average per year for this period.

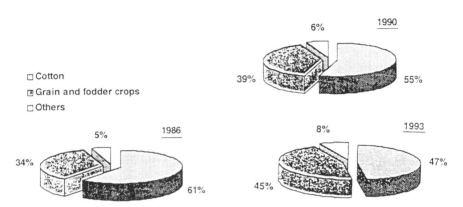

Fig. 4.5 **The composition of irrigated crops in Uzbekistan (as a percentage of total crop area) (Source: UNDP, 1995)**

cotton, grains, and fodder crops (such as alfalfa) and other crops in Uzbekistan.

Sealevel decline
The decline in the level of the Aral Sea has received considerable political attention both domestically and internationally. It is a highly noticeable environmental change, visible directly on the ground as well as from space. Water diversions from the two main regional rivers robbed the sea and deltas of annual freshwater replenishment. The rate of decline of the Sea can be seen in figure 4.6 (Micklin and Williams, 1996). Note also that declining levels were accompanied by an even more rapid decline in the volume of the Sea and by an increase in salinity.

It was not until the mid-1980s and *glasnost* that the Aral Sea situation took on the aura of an environmental catastrophe to many foreign observers. Although it was newly exposed to the international

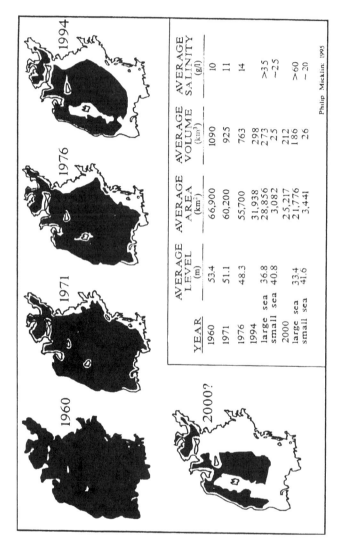

YEAR		AVERAGE LEVEL (m)	AVERAGE AREA (km²)	AVERAGE VOLUME (km³)	AVERAGE SALINITY (g/l)
1960		53.4	66,900	1090	10
1971		51.1	60,200	925	11
1976		48.3	55,700	763	14
1994			31,938	298	
	large sea	36.8	28,856	273	>35
	small sea	40.8	3,082	25	~25
2000			25,217	212	
	large sea	33.4	21,776	186	>60
	small sea	41.6	3,441	26	~20

Philip Micklin, 1995

Fig. 4.6 **Levels of the Aral Sea, 1960–2000 (Source: Micklin and Williams, 1996)**

media, and discussed with a new openness in the Soviet Union, it was, as suggested earlier, a known crisis situation that "crept up" on policy makers over a period of 30 years!

Related to declining sealevel and reduced sea surface area is the increase in the number and frequency of dust storms. In the mid-1970s, dust storms captured the attention of Soviet policy makers when cosmonauts, during one of their space missions, photographed major dust storms in the receding shoreline in the south-eastern part of the Aral Sea. Exposed seabed enabled winds to pick up dust laden with a variety of chemicals and carry it hundreds of kilometres from the original site. Farms downwind of these storms became covered with these dry depositions, and farmers claimed that the productivity of their land, as well as their health, were being adversely affected. Since then, the number and intensity of these dust storms along the continually newly exposed dry seabed have apparently increased. In fact, it was the appearance of major dust storms that exposed to Soviet leaders and the rest of the world the extent of human mismanagement of Central Asian rivers' waters.

Decreasing flows of the Amudarya and Syrdarya into the Aral Sea
The Amudarya supplies about 70 per cent of the water to the Aral Sea, more than twice the flow of the second major river in the region, the Syrdarya. From the early 1960s, the decline in Syrdarya flow was noticed, and by the late 1970s no Syrdarya water reached the Sea. As for the Amudarya, a sizeable amount of water is diverted from the river to the Karakum Canal (later the Lenin Canal and, today, the Niyazov Canal). The total amount diverted to this canal has been estimated at 15–20 km^3 per year, with diversions having increased at various stages of its completion. In the 1980s, there were a few years when virtually no Amudarya flow reached the Aral Sea. In recent years, however, as the result of favourable snowpack in the Pamir Mountains where the river has its origins, water has been reaching the Sea. The last leg of the Karakum Canal is completed, which will likely translate into the diversion of additional Amudarya water to the canal's extension to south-western Turkmenistan.

Before the rapid expansion of irrigated cotton production began in the 1960s in Uzbekistan and Turkmenistan, some Soviet scientists sought to alert their government to the possibility of a decline in sealevel decades into the future, as large volumes of water became increasingly diverted from the two major regional rivers that had historically determined the Sea's level.

Declining water quality in the rivers and in the Aral Sea
As fields were continually irrigated on a large scale, soil fertility rapidly declined. This prompted attempts to use increasing amounts of fertilizers, herbicides, and pesticides to maintain, if not expand, cotton productivity and production. Many of these chemicals found their way through the return flow to the rivers, as well as to the groundwater. In addition, to avoid (or really delay) the worsening of the salinization of soils, increasing amounts of water had to be used to flush the land of salts and other compounds. Much of this drainage water was returned to the rivers and, eventually, to the Sea. Drainage canals were eventually constructed to divert some of the contaminated water away from the Sea and into Lake Sarakamysh, a regional desert depression.

Degradation of the deltaic ecosystems
As another example of the ecological consequences of reduced streamflow into the sea, the degradation of the highly productive Amudarya and Syrdarya deltaic regions has become increasingly pronounced during the past 30 years (Smith, 1994). One of the consequences of the desiccation of the delta region has been the diminution of vegetative cover, a loss that destroyed habitats for wildlife and migratory birds. Frederick (1991, p. 12) highlighted the economic importance of the deltas in the recent past, noting that they provided a "feeding base for livestock, a source of reeds for industry, spawning grounds for fish, and sites of commercial hunting and trapping." Each of these delta-related ecological and societal processes has either been sharply curtailed or ended (Novikova, 1998).

Wildlife disappeared from around the delta and forests became decimated as the soils dried out or became salinized or waterlogged, depending on local soil conditions. Kuznetsov (1992, p. 324) supported this view of the early observation of adverse impacts, when he wrote that

the degradation of wetland soils in the deltas was noted quite clearly as early as the second half of the 1960s. For the preservation of the most fertile soils of the Amudarya delta, it was proposed that they be artificially irrigated, for which it was recommended that $3.0–3.5$ km^3/year of river water be used. However, professional water managers and land reclamation specialists paid no heed to this recommendation, nor to many others.

Today, political interest in the Aral Sea appears to have been reduced to the deltas of the Amudarya and Syrdarya. Supported by recommendations from the World Bank, Uzbek and Kazak leaders have proposed to rejuvenate deltaic ecosystems, abandoning the more ambitious schemes designed to save the entire Aral Sea, including the deltas.

Destruction of fish populations in the Aral Sea

With declining river water quality came a decline in the quality of Aral Sea water. At a 1977 Soviet conference on the environmental impact of a drop in the level of the Aral Sea, a paper prepared by two Uzbek republic scientists reported a sharp reduction in fish landings (Gorodetskaya and Kes, 1978). They suggested that a demise of the commercial fishery would likely occur because of the desiccation of the Sea's fish spawning grounds. Borovsky (1980) had also suggested that the depletion of the Aral Sea fisheries would be one of the first consequences of declining sealevels. Reteyum (1991, p. 3) wrote that "in 1965, the Council of Ministers of the USSR passed a special resolution, On Measures to Preserve the Fishery Importance of the Aral Sea." He cited this as one of the examples to support his belief that signs of deterioration in the Aral basin were seen as early as the mid-1960s.

The sharp decline in fish landings provided a visible threshold for decision makers to see that their inaction with regard to declining sealevel and water quality had its adverse biological consequences. By the late 1970s, it was quite clear that the Aral Sea fisheries were in an irreversible decline. A once-thriving fishing industry had become adversely affected by increasing amounts of pollutants entering the Sea by way of the river. The salinity of Aral Sea water increased to such an extent that several areas had the same salinity as the open ocean.

Today, no fish are caught commercially in the Sea; the Aral Sea ports of Muynak and Aralsk are now several tens of kilometres from the receding shoreline; and into the early 1990s fish had been shipped in from distant locations (the Arctic, the Baltic, the Pacific) for processing. The loss of fish productivity sparked a collapse of the industry and employment in this sector. In 1960, 43,430 metric tons of fish were caught in the Sea, dropping to 17,400 tons in 1970, to zero tons in 1980, and remaining there until now (Létolle and Mainguet, 1993, p. 182).

Increases in human diseases

The consequences of the dependence of several Central Asian republics on cotton monoculture not only adversely affected the physical environment by upsetting ecological balances in many parts of the Aral basin, but have also had a devastating impact on human health. Documented regional effects have only recently been exposed to the public: high infant mortality and morbidity rates, a sharp increase in oesophageal cancers directly attributable to "poisoned" water resources, gastro-intestinal problems, typhoid, high rates of congenital deformation, outbreaks of viral hepatitis, the contamination of mothers' milk, and a life expectancy in some areas about 20 years less than for the Commonwealth of Independent States (CIS) in general. Groundwater supplies, too, have been contaminated as a result of the widespread and wanton use of chemicals on irrigated cotton fields. By all statistical measures, the region's human health profile fares poorly in comparison with the rest of the CIS (Feshbach and Friendly, 1992; Ellis, 1990). Adverse impacts of all-out cotton production on health have been compounded by the absolute dearth of medical and health facilities in the Aral basin. In addition, water treatment facilities in the region are wholly inadequate (and in many areas non-existent), necessitating the use for domestic purposes of untreated surface waters from the rivers, irrigation canals, and drainage ditches.

Systematic research on public health in the Aral Sea basin began in the mid-1970s. From that time, the negative dynamics of deteriorating public health conditions in the region were observed. Had such research been systematically undertaken earlier, these adverse public health conditions would have been identified by the end of the 1960s, and would probably have been linked to the presence of pesticides (Elpiner, 1990, 1998). In addition, Kuznetsov (1992, p. 327) noted that "unfortunately, secrecy over an entire series of research results in the 1970s, especially medical-epidemiological data, precluded their publication at that time and the predictions associated with them did not become available to the public in time."

By way of illustration, one typical, tragic situation deserves mention, namely, the condition of the Karakalpak, the Turkic-speaking people of autonomous Karakalpakstan in north-west Uzbekistan. More than 1 million people have been affected:

There is a shortage of clean water, and there is not enough even for drinking. In several parts of the region the consumption of water per person per day is about 5 liters, compared to an average of 200 to 300 liters. The mineralization (salt content) of this water stands at 2 to 4 grams per liter, and the bacteria content exceeds the maximum permissible concentration by 5 to 10 times. Through the dispensary system the Ministry of Health discovered a truly tragic picture: 60 percent of those examined – children and adults – have serious health problems; 80 percent of pregnant women suffer from anemia; intestinal infections are widespread; the infant mortality rate is much higher than national average figures and in several regions reaches 82 in 1000 newborns. Diseases never before seen here are appearing, for example gallstones and kidney stones. (Rudenko, 1989, p. 44)

In the absence of any major improvement in regional health care or in detoxifying water and land resources in the Aral basin, the only way out for regional inhabitants, other than perpetuating the status quo, has been emigration. However, despite previous Soviet plans to encourage those most directly and most negatively affected (the people of Karakalpakstan) to migrate to areas outside Central Asia, few have opted to leave their homeland. Thus, with few meaningful actions to improve the health of the people or the environment in the Aral basin, the total sum of misery can only increase, because the region boasts an extremely high population growth rate ranging from 2.6 to 3.2 per cent. At such growth rates, a doubling of the present-day regional population of over 30 million to 60 million is expected in the early decades of the twenty-first century. The UN Development Programme is actively seeking to address some of the social issues that constrain capacity-building, which is so necessary for the long-term "sustainable use of water and land resources in the basin" (UNDP, 1996).

Concluding comments and a call for research

Clearly, we already possess a considerable amount of information about the Aral Sea basin and the various physical processes of environmental change and degradation. Signs of change were appearing everywhere throughout the first 20 years of the Aral Sea problem (1960–1980): wind erosion, salt-laden dust storms, destroyed fish spawning grounds, the collapse of the fisheries, secondary salinization, increased salinity of Sea water, waterlogging, disruption of navigation, the likely division of the Sea into separate parts, the need for extra-basin water resources to stabilize the Sea level, the loss of wildlife in the littoral areas, the large reduction of streamflow from the two main tributaries, a change in the regional climate, the disappearance of pasturelands, and so forth. Each one of these adverse environmental changes was mentioned in Soviet scientific literature at some point in the 1960s and 1970s.

It would be very instructive for scientific and societal reasons to focus on identifying and analysing various thresholds for awareness of and responses to each of these creeping environmental changes. The findings of such research can be used to aid national and international decision makers to develop more effective coping mechanisms for existing CEPs, to avert the development of future CEPs in the region. Those findings can be used to improve political as well as societal responses to CEPs not only in the Aral basin but elsewhere on the globe. One such effort of limited scope is presently under way (Glantz, 1998), but a larger, more comprehensive, and systematic effort is needed so that societies can identify and develop more effective response mechanisms to the creeping environmental changes that surround us.

Acknowledgement

The National Center for Atmospheric Research is sponsored by the National Science Foundation.

References

Bedford, D. P. 1996. "International water management in the Aral Sea basin." *Water International* 21, pp. 63–69.

Borovsky, V. M. 1980. "The drying out of the Aral Sea and its consequences." Scripta Publishing Co. (from *Izvestiya Akademii Nauk SSSR, seriya geograficheskaya*), No. 5.

Broecker, W. S. 1987. "Unpleasant surprises in the greenhouse?" *Nature* 328, pp. 123–126.

Burton, I. and K. Hewett. 1974. "Ecological dimensions of environmental hazards." In: F. Sargent (ed.), *Human Ecology*. Amsterdam: North-Holland, pp. 253–283.

Critchlow, J. 1991. *Nationalism in Uzbekistan: A Soviet Republic's Road to Sovereignty*. Boulder, Colo.: Westview Press.

Döös, B. R. 1994. "Why is environmental protection so slow?" *Global Environmental Change* 4(3), pp. 179–184.

Economist, The. 1991. "A way of life evaporates." 21 September, p. 59.

———— 1994. "No more caviar." 15 October, pp. 90–91.

Eickelman, D. F. (ed.). 1993. *Russia's Muslim Frontiers: New Directions in Cross-Cultural Analysis*. Bloomington, Ind.: Indiana University Press.

Ellis, W. S. 1990. "The Aral: A Soviet sea lies dying." *National Geographic*, February, p. 83.

Elpiner, L. I. 1990. "Medical-ecological problems in the eastern Aral region." Paper presented at University of Indiana conference on "The Aral Sea Crisis: Environmental Issues in Central Asia," Bloomington, Indiana, mimeo.

———— 1998. "Public health in the Aral Sea coastal region and the dynamics of changes in the ecological situation." In: M. H. Glantz (ed.), *Creeping Environ-*

mental Problems and Sustainable Development in the Aral Sea Basin. Cambridge: Cambridge University Press, in press.

Feshbach, M. and A. Friendly Jr. 1992. *Ecocide in the USSR: Health and Nature under Siege*. New York: Basic Books.

Frederick, K. D. 1991. "The disappearing Aral Sea." *Resources*, Winter, pp. 11–14.

Glantz, M. H. 1994. "Creeping environmental phenomena: Are societies equipped to deal with them?" Paper presented at "Creeping Environmental Phenomena and Societal Responses to Them," Boulder, Colo., 7–10 February.

——— (ed.). 1998. *Creeping Environmental Problems and Sustainable Development in the Aral Sea Basin*. Cambridge: Cambridge University Press, in press.

Glantz, M. H. and I. Zonn. 1991. "A quiet Chernobyl." *The World & I*, September, pp. 324–329.

Glantz, M. H., A. Z. Rubinstein, and I. Zonn. 1993. "Tragedy in the Aral Sea basin: Looking back to plan ahead?" *Global Environmental Change* 3(2), pp. 174–198.

Gore, A. 1992. *Earth in the Balance: Ecology and the Human Spirit*. Boston: Houghton Mifflin.

Gorodetskaya, M. Ye. and A. S. Kes. 1978. "Alma-Ata conference on the environmental impact of a drop in the level of the Aral Sea." *Soviet Geography* 19(10), pp. 728–736.

Hoffer, E. 1952. *The Ordeal of Change*. New York: Harper & Row.

Jamieson, D. 1991. "The epistemology of climate change: Some morals for managers." *Society and Natural Resources* 4, pp. 319–329.

Kahneman, D., P. Slovic, and A. Tversky. 1982. *Judgment under Uncertainty: Heuristics and Biases*. Cambridge: Cambridge University Press.

Kasperson, J. et al. 1995. *Regions at Risk: Comparisons of Threatened Environments*. Tokyo: UNU Press.

Kuznetsov, N. T. 1992. "Geographical and ecological aspects of Aral Sea hydrological functions." *Post-Soviet Geography* 33(5).

Létolle, R. and M. Mainguet. 1993. *Aral*. Paris: Springer-Verlag.

Micklin, P. and W. D. Williams (eds.). 1996. *The Aral Sea Basin*. NATO ASI Series 2: Environment, vol. 12. Berlin: Springer-Verlag, pp. 5–6.

Novikova, N. 1998. "Creeping environmental changes in the pre-Aral ecosystems under the Aral Sea crisis. In: M. H. Glantz (ed.), *Creeping Environmental Problems and Sustainable Development in the Aral Sea Basin*. Cambridge: Cambridge University Press, in press.

O'Dy, S. 1991. "La voix du désert d'Aral." *L'Express*, August, pp. 52–55.

Orechkine, D. 1990. "La mer d'Aral menacée de disparition." *La Recherche 226* 21, November, pp. 1380–1388.

Palm, R. I. 1990. "Introduction to the study of natural hazards". In: R. I. Palm, *Natural Hazards*. Baltimore, Md: Johns Hopkins University Press, pp. 1–17.

Parisi, P. and M. H. Glantz. 1992. "Deforestation and public policy." *The World & I*, November, pp. 270–277.

Petterson, J. 1995. "The social component of (adaptive) ecological characterizations." Memo presented at NOAA Scientific Advisory Meeting on Adaptive Ecological Management, National Center for Atmospheric Research, Boulder, Colo., 9–10 March.

Rashid, A. 1994. *The Resurgence of Central Asia: Islam or Nationalism?* Karachi: Oxford University Press.

Reteyum, A. U. 1991. "Letter in Overview Section." *Environment* 33(1).

Rudenko, B. 1989. "Solenye Peski Aralkum [The salty sands of the Aral]." *Nauka i zhizn* 10, October, p. 44.

Smith, D. 1994. "Change and variability in climate and ecosystem decline in Aral Sea Basin deltas." *Post-Soviet Geography* 35(3), pp. 142–165.

Tucker, C. J., H. E. Dregne, and W. W. Newcomb. 1991. "Expansion and contraction of the Sahara Desert from 1980 to 1990." *Science* 253, pp. 299–301.

UNDP (United Nations Development Programme). 1995. *Uzbekistan: Human Development Report 1995.* Tashkent, Uzbekistan: UNDP.

—— 1996. *Tentative Strategy for UNDP's Contribution to the Aral Sea Program.* UNDP/EC-ICAS, Version 3, 3 April, mimeo.

UNU (United Nations University). 1992. *Environmental Management of the Aral Sea Region.* Report of the International Symposium held at UNU Headquarters, Tokyo, Japan, 29 September 1992. Global Infrastructure Fund Research Foundation Japan.

5

The Aral Sea and socio-economic development

Tsuneo Tsukatani

Introduction

The states of Central Asia have once again appeared on the international stage, abandoning the 70-year experiment of Soviet socialism. What is happening there today is, as has happened since the dawn of history, also sure to decide the fate of humans. States in this region are facing a serious economic crisis. These states consist of more than 100 ethnic groups, possess large numbers of conventional and nuclear weapons, face Islamic countries to the south, and lie midway between China and Europe. Lack of economic progress could easily lead to serious conflicts within and between these countries.

In addition, Central Asia is facing serious environmental problems. These problems, mostly started in the early 1960s, head the list of global environmental problems in that their size and the difficulty of solving them are unparalleled elsewhere in the world. Many people, including leaders of the states, however, are more concerned about "business" than about sustainable development that meets the needs not only of the present generations but also of future ones. The transition to a market-oriented economy will take many years, but the victims of the environmental disruption are dying day by day and the people are suffering.

This chapter seeks to identify what kind of political and economic structure caused the environmental disruption, and to show that what lies behind the discrepancy between desire and reality is the same as what caused the environmental disruption.

The technical system of cotton monoculture

A cry of despair

In June 1984, the 16th Plenary Session of the Uzbekistan Communist Party Central Committee uttered a cry of despair:

In the first three years of the last five-year plan, of the 44 enterprises and production facilities put into operation during this time, half are experiencing considerable delays in reaching their rated capacity. Dozens of machine tools stand idle because of a lack of relatively insignificant parts.

In the past few years the Ministry of the Cotton-Processing Industry has not fulfilled its plans, fiber output has declined, fiber quality has deteriorated, and waste and losses of raw cotton have grown. Report-padding and persistent theft have become widespread. Demoralization has set in among many categories of personnel, including certain executives of the ministry, enterprises and procurement stations. Paper transactions have been carried out on a large scale, and bribery has flourished.

In the past few years, cotton mills and procurement stations in Tashkent region have violated standard requirements when accepting raw cotton, and indices for moisture and impurity content have been understated. As a result, the Tashkent Cotton Procurement and Production Association is not ensuring the planned output of fiber and is allowing extensive overconsumption of raw cotton and large amounts of waste.

Whereas in 1980 one hectare of plowed land produced 1,337 rubles' worth of output, last year productivity fell to 1,241 rubles' worth. Mistakes are still being made in the design, construction and operation of irrigation systems, and the area of unused arable land increased from 4,000 hectares in 1975 to 67,000 hectares in 1983. Because of mismanagement and disregard for technical and economic calculations, newly created state farms in Khorezm and a number of other provinces are operating inefficiently. Mismanagement has led to the disuse of land after a single harvest in the Makhankulsky, Urtachulsky, Varakhshinsky and Shakhrisabz tracts. Their reconstruction will require millions of additional rubles.

Corruption in the social system produces the stagnation of technology, and then the stagnation of technology leads to further corruption of the social system, and so on. In the former Soviet Union, where there were plenty of resources such as oil, metals, water, and labour, the only resource that had been exhausted was the development of civilian technology and a social system that stimulates technological development. It was stagnation of agricultural technology that promoted corruption in cotton production and the depletion of the Aral Sea.

The level of mechanization

The level of mechanization of cotton agriculture was extremely low and inefficient. Even in the harvesting season of 1984, which occurred after the 16th Plenary Session mentioned above, 17,000 harvesting machines out of 37,000 were completely unused. Up until 1980, more than 3.5 million metric tons of raw cotton were harvested by machine, nearly two-thirds of the total volume. In 1984, however, only 1.5 million metric tons of cotton were picked by machine, which represented only 44 per cent for the whole of Uzbekistan. Many collective and state farms harvested just 5 to 20 per cent of their crops by machine. On the farms of the Bukhara region, each machine accounted for 5 tons of harvested cotton, i.e. each machine operated for an average of two days in 1984. There were also farms where harvesting equipment was not used at all.

Irrigation technology

Irrigation technology was far from an automated system. Of the 19 million hectares of irrigated land in the former USSR, just over 7 million hectares were equipped with sprinklers. The remaining area relied on surface irrigation, where water is channelled into furrows by means of gravity. In almost all cases, this was done manually, using shovels and hoes, wasting a great deal of time and energy. The irrigation equipment of the Uzbek state and collective farms comprises nearly 150,000 machines. But they no longer fully meet present requirements. In the late 1970s, the first models of the Kuban broad-swath sprinkler were introduced, at a cost 400 per cent higher than that of the old machines. Another machine, the DDN-70 unit, washed away up to 30 tons of soil per hectare, removing the fertile topsoil and more than half the seeds along with it.

The workforce

The workforce was poorly organized. There are many in the Ministry of Agriculture's departments and administrations who have absolutely no specialist knowledge or understanding of agriculture's needs and who have neither work experience nor higher-level agricultural diplomas. For example, in Bukhara Oblast, 20 per cent of the collective farm chairmen and 40 per cent of the state farm directors did not have an agricultural education. In the same oblast, two or three city people came to harvest cotton for every collective farmer and state farm worker. On the Maxim Gorky Collective Farm in Altyaryk District, the collective farmers harvested 905 metric tons of raw cotton; each picker handed over an average of 1,400 kg of cotton to the raw-cotton mill. On the same farm, the outsiders who came to help picked 1,328 tons of raw cotton, each of them accounting for an average of 2,500 kg of raw cotton. Machines on that farm picked only 3 per cent of the total.

No concept of cost

Estimates suggest that 1.5 million farmers were involved in raising cotton. If each of them were to work 33 days in a season to harvest just 60 kg a day, they could hand-pick more than 3 million tons of cotton. If each one of the 37,000 picking machines were to collect 80 tons in one season, another 3 million tons of cotton could be collected. The real situation was completely different from this, however. The reason is clear; there was no concept of cost. In 1987, a collective farmer was paid just 8 kopeks per kg of hand-picked cotton. But city residents, in addition to regular daily wages averaging 8.5 rubles, received not only 10 kopeks per kg from the farm, but another 20 kopeks per kg from their regular employer. Aside from whether they were really paid, even students made 30 kopeks per kg. Meanwhile, the farmer had to harvest his private crops, and the profit he made from selling his products at the market accounted for a sizeable part of his family's income; it dwarfed what he would make from harvesting cotton. Instead of going out in the fields, the adults travelled to market to sell their privately grown produce or to make the rounds of the shops.

Cotton processing

There are also many problems at the stage of cotton processing. In the summer of 1960, when a Japanese delegation from the textile machine industry visited Tashkent, among other places, it reported that the general level of machinery was the same as that of Japan of

15 years earlier (Izumi, 1960). This meant that their technology had not changed since the end of World War II. The same comment can be applied to contemporary technology as well. The most serious problem lies in cotton-processing technology, because it proved unable to handle the massive volume of machine-harvested cotton, which has more moisture and impurities than hand-harvested cotton. The cotton-processing period has been much longer than that in other countries, starting in August and ending in mid-June of the next year. It was claimed that this reduced the seasonal variation in labour work and provided workers with stable conditions. But the real reason was a shortage of capacity in processing plants for ginning. Procurement centres are also running short of the machinery necessary to dry cotton. The ratio of fibre production to raw cotton of the first-grade quality in Uzbekistan decreased from 34.1 per cent to 30.2 per cent (Izahara, 1990).

Textile industry

Although Uzbekistan is the fifth-largest producer of cotton in the world, it has virtually no textile industry of its own. Only 12 per cent of the country's cotton production is processed domestically. The European Bank for Reconstruction and Development, the World Bank, and the German Hermes fund, as well as several firms from Turkey, Japan, and other countries have offered to help Uzbekistan modernize cotton production and establish its own textile industry. To modernize its industry, Uzbekistan will need no less than US$1 billion before the year 2000. A policy oriented towards developing a domestic processing industry and a radical change in cotton-growing technology and soil treatment is expected to have its first results in five to seven years. Specialists calculate that, if the planned set of measures were fully implemented, the share of domestically processed cotton would rise to 20 per cent, allowing Uzbekistan to become a leader among the world's textile exporters.

The cotton swindle

Sharaf Rashidov, 1959 to 1983

If we are to speak about cotton and irrigation in the former Soviet Union, we must not forget Sharaf Rashidov, the late First Secretary of the Uzbekistan Communist Party Central Committee. He held the position from 1959 until his death in 1983. Before and after he became the First Secretary, internal strife was horrendous, and it was only in 1971 that Rashidov succeeded in filling the chairmanship of the Republic Council of Ministers and of the Presidium of the Uzbekistan Supreme Soviet with his followers (Carlisle, 1986). An organized state crime group, the so-called Uzbek mafia, was formed around this time. Crime usually involves a cross-section of society, but the activity of the Uzbek mafia demonstrates the real situation in contemporary Central Asia and its future. Rashidov understood clearly what was required of a republic leader, and managed to present himself in the Kremlin's corridors of power as a man personally devoted to General Secretary Brezhnev. The cotton monoculture was the creation of Rashidov himself. A sharp deterioration in irrigated land did not stop the continuous increase in the Five-Year Plan, and gave rise to report-padding. The embezzlement of federal money, acquired by report-padding, automatically increased the annual procurement targets. Every figure went on increasing, even though it was clear that the farmers could not achieve the procurement plan. Because the plan's targets had to be met, an atmosphere was gradually created that encouraged report-padding on a massive scale.

Not quality but quantity

It was not the quantity and quality of ginned cotton (lint) but the weight of raw cotton that was inspected at the procurement centre to set the price of cotton. Report-padding was an everyday occurrence. Invoices were issued, with no goods backing them up, in order to acquire money from Moscow. The percentage of moisture or of "make weight" stones was understated. But there were still huge shortfalls in the ginning process. So it was also necessary to conceal the shortfalls in the ginning process, and this was done by any means to hand. This explains a paradox: the cotton harvest had been growing, whereas fabric production had been decreasing. Shortfalls of 0.5 to 1 million metric tons had to be produced every year on paper, for which the state paid. The money rarely went to those who toiled in the fields. It disappeared along the way, with the aid of fake work orders and paylists and fictitious persons, creating a "cash box" to fund future bribes at reception centres. In this way, a vicious circle came into being: report-padding, then embezzlement, then bribes. In Uzbekistan questions were never resolved without a bribe. Anyone offering a bribe got what they wanted. The outcome was greed, abuse of office for mercenary motives, a lack of supervision, immorality, mutual protection, graft, unscrupulousness, favouritism by geographical origin, nepotism, suppression of subordinates' initiative, and trying to please higher-ups.

The structure of the swindle

Because such matters were under the jurisdiction of the Ministry of Internal Affairs, Rashidov selected as his main target Mr. Churbanov, a son-in-law of Brezhnev. Churbanov rose to become First Deputy Minister of Internal Affairs early in 1980. One of Brezhnev's close associates, Shchelokov, who was the USSR Minister of Internal Affairs, was also chosen as a member of the Uzbek mafia. Uzbekistan's Minister of Internal Affairs and three deputy ministers, directors of provincial internal affairs administrations, joined it too. All affairs were controlled by these actors. This was a systematic crime in the socialist state where quantity, not the quality, was the only thing that was evaluated. It was not until 1984 that quality was taken into account for payment (Juurokuhara, 1985). This explains why the formal statistics for the cotton harvest decreased suddenly in 1984. In the previous year, investigations started for the first time, and revealed that the republic's statistics before 1984 were a fiction. The investigations revealed that between 1978 and 1983 alone 4.5 million tons of raw cotton were produced on paper only. This cost the state 4 billion rubles (US$6.7 billion) in total, half of which went into the pockets of the leaders.

The start of investigations

Brezhnev died in November 1982. His successor, Andropov, who had been the Chairman of the KGB, dismissed Minister Shchelokov and began to investigate the crimes. He believed that socialism would more likely develop if scandals were exposed. Uzbekistan was the main target for Andropov and the KGB. A team from the USSR Prosecutor's Office started an investigation of Uzbek corruption in 1983. Though Rashidov was partly successful at that time in removing the leaders of the republic's KGB, thus isolating the USSR Prosecutor's team, Andropov succeeded in exposing the USSR Ministry of Internal Affairs. One day in 1983, First Deputy Prime Minister Aliyev, who was the chairman of the Azerbaijan KGB, from Moscow, visited Rashidov in Tashkent to pass on Andropov's tacit message. The next day, Rashidov suddenly died. Then, the Uzbek affair took a new turn, as the investigations spread through the whole country. Usmankhodzhayev, Rashidov's successor, vowed at the funeral that Uzbekistan would keep Rashidov's pledge to produce 6 million metric tons of raw cotton. He was able to do this by ordering the chairman of Uzbekistan's Council of Ministers to pad the figures by another 240,000 tons. All told, nearly 1 million tons of non-existent cotton were "produced" that year. When the cotton swindle in Uzbekistan was exposed, 18,000 people were expelled from the Party, and 330 people from the Ministry of Internal Affairs and the Prosecutor's Office, along with 600 leaders of the government and the Party, were prosecuted. However, the social structure did not change.

The aftermath

No one ever expected to be punished for the crime. Though the Party expelled those who confessed to their crimes and removed them from their jobs, those who kept quiet continued to enjoy security and comfort. It is a contradiction for the Party to investigate itself, in that it controls everything (Tishkov, 1991). Proving bribery was almost impossible. The crude investigation, which was peculiar to the Soviet Union, was not enough to prove a swindle protected by the strong and secret organization of the Party mafia. Some key personnel were sentenced to death without the structure of the criminal activity being clarified, and some committed suicide. Every piece of criminal evidence was lost. When leading officials in the Kremlin were to be investigated, the prosecutors were ordered to stop. Some of the prosecutors had political ambitions and were standing for election. In the end, the investigation, which gave priority to confession, disintegrated completely. The decision was taken to transfer the case to Tashkent after republic President Islam Karimov appealed to the USSR Supreme Court, noting that it was necessary to take into consideration the "specific character of the republic and the existing realities." Even Churbanov, Brezhnev's former son-in-law, was released in 1993 on the decree of Yeltsin. Others involved in this crime had been released a long time ago. Nobody knows how the Russian decree was issued, who initiated it, and why. Sharaf Rashidov, whose name is increasingly heard, was also re-established in 1993 as a national hero of Uzbekistan. It means that President Karimov has to continue an Asian autocracy to keep the economy stable – as long as he keeps the old regime.

Environmental problems and human health

Infant mortality

Infant mortality (the number of infant deaths under one year of age per 1,000 births) is an important indicator of the degree of maturity of a society. Data on deaths, specifically infant mortality, were among the greatest secrets in the former Soviet Union. Figures were first disclosed in 1986 after Gorbachev began his *glasnost* campaign, allowing more openness in society. However, international criteria have not yet been adopted with respect to statistical methods, and the figures could be double or triple. It is evident that Central Asia is now confronted with highly adverse circumstances on a scale unparalleled elsewhere in the world.

Uzbekistan

It has been reported that in the Karakalpak republic of Uzbekistan 11 per cent of all babies born there die before they are one year old – one of the highest infant mortality rates in Asia. It is also reported that two-thirds of people there suffer from hepatitis, typhoid or throat cancer, and that 83 per cent of children have serious illnesses. Among people of all ages, cases of infectious hepatitis, jaundice, and gastro-intestinal disease have multiplied. Malnutrition, anaemia, rickets, and even leprosy have reappeared.

Kazakhstan

Kazakhstan is in the same situation. In the 1970s and 1980s it showed a 3–29-fold rise in total morbidity for various infectious and somatic diseases associated with the drastic worsening of the ecological situation in the Aral Sea region. Child and maternal mortality rates have significantly increased. Investigations at the Institute for Regional Nutritional Problems of the USSR Academy of Medical Sciences have shown that pesticides, mineral fertilizers, and various micro-organisms and their toxic metabolites are major pollutants of food products in all Kazakhstan regions (Sharmanov, 1989). The important role played by nutritional status in showing the carcinogenic effect of nitro compounds must be established. A complex of measures aimed at improving state sanitary control over the environment and food products must also be elaborated. It must be noted that environmental degradation in Central Asia is directly connected not only with irrigation but also with dirty industries. Radioactive pollution in Leninabad (Uzbekistan) and Maili Sai (Kyrgyzstan), and heavy metal air pollution in Chimkent (Kazkahstan), among others, are all connected to the Aral Sea problem, but they must be solved separately.

Turkmenistan

The situation in Turkmenistan is much worse. In 1989, 125,054 infants were born and 6,846 died under the age of one (a mortality of 54.74/1,000). Stores in Takhta District, which is located along the right bank of the Amudarya, have not sold butter, meat, or chicken for the past 10 years. Some 85 per cent of families in the district do not have their own livestock and, therefore, it is very difficult to buy meat, milk, and dairy products even in the market. In some families, especially large ones, children are dying of starvation. In many rural areas of Turkmenistan, the autocratic state which was thought to have prevailed until the beginning of this century still exists. Among the chairmen of Turkmenian collective farms there are quite a few who behave like absolute rulers, masters of people's fates within their territory. No one has the right there to marry without their consent. Turkmenistan produces two and a half times as much raw cotton per capita as Tajikistan. Production of cotton, both per capita and as a proportion of the arable land, is the highest in Central Asia. This explains the acute shortage of foodstuffs, rising social tension, chronic hunger, and high infant mortality. Hereditary diseases – autosomal recessive (or latent) – may be another cause of high infant mortality. Intra-family marriages (most often between cousins) are common in Turkmenistan, sometimes accounting for 10 per cent or more of the total, and in some places accounting for 60 per cent. The economic reason for these blood ties is bride price ("*kalym*"). Those who demand and pay a bride price and those who keep a young woman confined in her father's house after the 40-day "honeymoon" until the husband's relatives pay the bride price in full (which can take years) are rarely punished.

Infection

Even highly educated leading medical doctors need to understand the role of infection in modern medicine. The direct cause of any disease ending in death is attributable to infection. No matter what kind of modern and high-tech medical equipment and medicines are introduced into Central Asia from Western countries, they will be either useless or dangerous to patients if public and medical concern about infection is not heightened. Mothers are quite often the carriers of infection and their babies die of intra-uterine septicaemia.

It has been very difficult to establish the real reasons why children are getting sick and dying in Central Asia. Doctors have most often diagnosed the problem as pneumonia, which is hard to disprove. People used to believe that their children died of pneumonia. In fact, these deaths were most often caused by infectious diseases, particularly intestinal infections that can be prevented. However, if the deaths can be blamed on pneumonia, then no one is responsible and no additional facilities or services have to be established. Only 40 per cent of the republic's population has a piped water supply. The rest use water from irrigation canals and ditches. This affects not just villages or small towns. Cities, even in Tashauz, have no sewerage systems. Where there is a water purification plant, the equipment is not properly maintained.

The problem of pesticide pollution

Pollution of water and soil

The catastrophe of the Aral Sea can be summarized in one word: cotton. For years, huge overdoses of chemical fertilizers, pesticides, and defoliants have been poured onto the cotton fields. Among them were DDT, BHC, methyl mercaptophos, octamethyl, butifos, milbex, hexachlorane (BHO), phosphamide (dimethoate), phosalone, lenacil, ronit (Ro-Neet), yalan (molinate), sodium TCA, chlorazone, and aldrin. The chemicals are not only discharged into the rivers through drainage canals, but have also filtered through to the groundwater layer when the salinated land is flushed by huge amounts of irrigation water, thus creating capillary channels between surface water and groundwater. The capillary action carries groundwater containing minerals and chemicals to the surface, where they are left to accumulate after the evaporation of the water. The groundwater itself also carries chemicals to the lower part of the river basin, where people are forced to use it for drinking and cooking.

In Uzbekistan, an average of 146.8 kg of chemical fertilizer in 1965, 238.3 kg in 1975, and 305.6 kg in 1987 was applied to each hectare of agricultural land, whereas the figure was 122.1 kg in 1987 for the whole USSR. Pesticides and herbicides too were dumped onto the cotton fields of Uzbekistan. In 1980, for example, 121,400 tons of chemicals were used. In the late 1970s, the total amount was between 30 and 35 kg per hectare on Uzbekistan's cultivated land, almost 30 times higher than the average for the whole USSR.

Butifos and its history

Butifos (*S, S, S-tributyl-trithiophosphate*; (C4H9S)3PO) is similar to the American preparations Folex and DEF. It was recommended for use in 1964 on the initiative of the USSR Ministry of the Chemical Industry and the USSR Ministry of Agriculture's State Commission on Chemical Herbicides and Pesticides, with the consent of the USSR Ministry of Public Health but with incomplete data on its toxicity. Butifos acts on the human body by affecting the central nervous system, the heart, the liver, and the kidneys and disturbing immunological reactivity, especially in children. The nauseating stench from the fields creeps over villages and suburbs, causing a sharp deterioration in the way residents feel, and sometimes leading to dangerous allergic reactions. In 1983, finally responding to the demands of the republic's physicians and scientists, the USSR Ministry of Public Health banned the use of butifos in agriculture altogether. But it reserved the right to authorize its use in certain campaigns and in certain republics at the request of interested departments. In 1984 roughly 70 per cent of Uzbekistan's fields were treated with butifos, and in 1985 the figure was still about 60 per cent.

Substitutes and intoxication

Substitutes appeared as early as 1965. The Institute of Chemistry of the Uzbek Academy of Sciences developed a less toxic, inexpensive, and sufficiently effective defoliant based on calcium cyanamide. Its proposal was rejected by the Ministry of Agriculture, which claimed that the republic was already supplied with an "effective" defoliant. By the late 1970s, another preparation was developed in the republic that was superior to butifos in every way and was still only slightly toxic. This preparation, known as UDM, underwent the prescribed tests and in 1980 received the approval of the highest authority – the USSR Ministry of Agriculture's State Commission on Chemical Herbicides and Pesticides. It was only in March 1987, however, that the USSR Ministry of Public Health banned the production and usage of butifos.

With regard to the health status of schoolchildren living in a rural area of Uzbekistan, a high proportion of diseases of the nervous system and mental disorders may be associated with chronic pesticide intoxication (Khalmetov and Beketova, 1993). It has been noted that in regions where toxic chemicals are intensively used children exhibit a significant decrease in phagocytic activity of leukocytes (Sadikova et al., 1990). Examinations of the eyes of 5–14-year-old children living near fields and exposed to pesticides revealed significant increases in intra-ocular pressure and in humour production (Khamdamov, 1976). Water samples from different sources to the south of the Aral Sea region indicate the ability to induce chromosomal abnormalities in the somatic and sexual cells of mammals (Zakhidov et al., 1993). A four-fold increase in chromosomal rearrangement and a five-fold increase in polychromatophilic erythrocytes with micronuclei were found in the bone marrow of wild mice caught in cotton fields subjected to intensive application of various pesticides (Khalikov, 1990).

The environment of the Aral Sea and international cooperation

Overview of the situation

The Uzbek Academy of Sciences says that a new desert has been created to the south and east of the Aral Sea, and has already expanded to 5 million hectares. It is spreading more rapidly across Central Asian countries than the Sahara desert. The new desert, which is expanding at the rate of 150,000 hectares every year, could be called a "white desert" because the toxic salt pans encrust its surface after merging with the Karakum (black desert), Kyzylkum (red desert), and other deserts.

Fishing villages once on the shore are now between 30 and 80 km from the shoreline. All sea life has died, and fishing communities have been destroyed. When I visited Bugun, once a fishing village at the mouth of Syrdarya, in 1991, former fishermen were working in factories smoking and packing sea fish. The fish came from distant Atlantic fisheries such as Murmansk by train with no concern for the cost. This was an unemployment policy on a large scale at the end of the Soviet Union.

The cooling effect that the sea used to have on the hot summers of Central Asia has diminished, cutting rainfall and accelerating desertification processes in the region. Chemicals used on irrigated fields drain into the Sea, sink to the seabed, and form toxic salt pans as the

Sea dries. The chemicals are then lifted into the atmosphere by winds and later fall on the area in rain, causing high rates of infant mortality and sickness. Eight or nine times a year, dust storms drop 5 million tons of salt, sand, and dust on Central Asia. The sky becomes obscured by a salty curtain, and the sun turns crimson and disappears behind the salt dust. Not one tree grows on the land, and livestock are perishing. The people, too, get sick and die.

Two views on the fate of the Aral Sea

The conclusion may be that the regeneration of the Aral Sea is not an option because far greater economic benefit can be derived from the use of river water for irrigation than from its runoff into the Aral Sea. This view is economic and technocratic and does not take into account a whole range of factors that support the view that the Sea should be preserved. The Sea has played a role in fisheries and transportation, and has supported the life of people there. Nor is it possible fully to estimate the consequences for nature and the economy of any human intervention that assumes the non-economic importance of the Aral Sea. The moral responsibility of our generation to preserve this vulnerable and unique natural legacy for our descendants is of greater importance. Moreover, we have just started to evaluate the *total* effect of cotton monoculture on nature and the economy. Several ways of dealing with the Aral Sea problem have emerged.

Coping with the Aral Sea problem

Gigantomania

One long-standing scheme is to divert the waters of such Siberian rivers as the Ob, Irtysh, and Yenisey and to channel them southward to the Aral Sea region and to the desert. This reminds us of the words of Ivan Michurin: "We cannot wait for favors from nature; our task is to seize them from her" (Davydov, 1949). This plan has been cancelled after years of controversy about its cost and environmental consequences, but some local scientists are still hanging on to the idea. Another suggestion was to break up the glaciers of the Pamir and Tien Shan mountains with nuclear explosions. The Amudarya, in its turn, would be topped up by water from the River Indus. Other plans include the construction of a water intake on the River Kabul, from which a pipeline would cross Pakistan and Afghanistan. These ideas may be tainted by gigantomania and are not realistic, especially at a time of economic crisis. However, such ideas are sure to survive.

Blame Moscow

A second reaction is to blame Moscow for ignorance and corruption. Central planners in Moscow no doubt calculated that by massive irrigation they could simultaneously develop their backward southern regions, provide enough jobs for the indigenous people, and have them serve Russia. Almost all the raw cotton was sent north for processing, and successive five-year plans required still more irrigated land. Because the plan provided the wrong incentives, quality and yields started to fall in 1980. People in the affected area – about 35 million of them – started to realize how much cotton slavery had diminished their lives. Moscow, suggesting that their hardship was their own fault, then sent a group of prosecutors and KGB to accuse local leaders of ignorance, mismanagement, and corruption. Even Gorbachev himself once criticized Uzbekistan for squandering water and not pulling its weight. Until the independence of the republics, the intellectuals of the region – especially writers and scientists – were less willing to let the citizens of Central Asia take all the blame. Since independence, it has been clear that it is the citizens of Central Asia who have to suffer the hardships and pains.

A business-as-usual strategy

In the first four years of the 1980s, the Uzbek Agro-Industrial Complex received 10 billion rubles from Moscow. Between 1966 and 1984, 21 billion rubles were invested in the development of the water resources of Uzbekistan. A considerable amount of this money was spent on bribery. In the irrigated area of Central Asia, which comprises more than 9.4 million hectares, part of the drainage network did not function. This, together with too little attention to crop rotation, led to the salinization of large areas. As a result, the area sown to alfalfa decreased, while cotton became the single crop. This has led to a situation in which soil fertility has fallen off, the incidence of cotton-plant disease has increased, and the volume and quality of the harvest have declined.

In each republic, farmers are seeking their own solutions. Some are directing the drainage flow into the desert and natural depressions in the steppe. The local soils are mostly light-textured and very permeable to water. This anarchic dumping of drainage water is raising the groundwater level, creating additional problems for both rural and urban people. Several lakes have appeared that are making pastureland boggy and encouraging insects. Moreover, the salty and poisonous water seeps into the ground, and gets into freshwater wells. But every well, even the smallest, is very valuable. Uzbek President Islam Karimov first urged international cooperation to save the Aral Sea on the 60th anniversary of the city of Nukus in December 1992, but he has not yet addressed the question of cutting back cotton cultivation, which consumes the most water but also supplies 80 per cent of the nation's hard currency earnings. Turkmenistan, a desert land entirely dependent on water from the Amudarya, embarked on a new irrigation plan in 1993 which envisages the cultivation of 1.6 million hectares. Turkmenistan's Minister of Water Economy and Supply has said that it is impossible to save the Aral Sea and that it will become a dry, dead sea in 30 years. Turkmenistan's Minister for Agriculture and Food claims that the project is a national priority, intended to achieve self-sufficiency in grain and other crops. These plans reflect the behaviour of those who have few ideas about what to do other than to pursue a business-as-usual strategy.

Involve international society
Cooperation with international society is the only way to cope with the environmental problems in this area. The first conference of heads of state in Central Asia on the problems of the Aral Sea was held in Kzyl-Orda in March of 1993, with the participation of the Russian Deputy Premier. The conference set up an International Aral Foundation (IAF) and an Inter-State Council for the Aral Basin headed by Nursultan Nazarbayev, Kazakhstan's President. Each of the IAF member countries was to contribute 1 per cent of its GNP annually to the Foundation. The conference also adopted an appeal to the United Nations. In January 1994, the leaders of Kazakhstan, Uzbekistan, Turkmenistan, and Kyrgyzstan pledged to pay 1 per cent of their 1994 budgets into the fund (in Tajikistan the government faces a more severe crisis of civil war). Few financial statistics for each country are available, but Kazakhstan's GDP for 1994 was around 464.5 billion tenge and its national budget was around 80 billion tenge, and 1 per cent of these figures is US$72 million and US$12 million, respectively. The figures for Uzbekistan are US$10 billion for GDP and US$4 billion for national revenue, making the 1 per cent figures US$100 million and US$40 million, respectively.

Unfortunately, none of these countries was able to fulfil its pledge.

Instead, responding to the setting-up of the IAF and the preceding appeal of the leaders, international organizations and foreign countries proposed financial and technical aid. In February 1993, the European Bank for Reconstruction and Development prepared to provide technical and financial aid for environmental conservation projects in the area around the Aral Sea. In April, the German Red Cross decided to donate a water purification plant to Karakalpak victims. In May, Germany proposed DM 1.3 million for a comprehensive environmental survey and for water and soil research at the mouths of the Amudarya and Syrdarya rivers. In September, President Mitterand of France expressed his intention to participate in the Save Aral Project. US Secretary of State Warren Christopher promised a US$140 million aid package in October 1994, US$15 million of which was to improve the environment around the Aral Sea and the Semipalatinsk nuclear testing area. It was reported in January 1994 that India would give Uzbekistan US$500,000. Japan also pledged financial and technical aid in April 1994. The World Bank, having spent two years studying the problem, embarked on the development of costly projects. For the preparation of the programme, the World Bank granted US$41 million to the fund in November 1994.

The future of Central Asia

Cotton culture

Cotton is an important crop in the world. Its fibre is clean and it involves various fields of industry. It is an important crop in Central Asia because the production of synthetic fibres may pollute the environment. Most importantly, however, cotton can earn valuable hard currency in export markets. If Central Asia were to produce value-added "white gold," then cotton would surely be a winner in the world market. Uzbekistan, though it hopes to extend its cotton trade with foreign countries, lacks trading experience. Moreover, world cotton prices do not favour Central Asian producers. The cotton harvest is still falling, partly because the area under cultivation has been reduced in favour of grain production, but mainly because of the irrational use of harvesting machinery and because of shortages of fuel and spare parts. There still exist many technical and social barriers to a breakthrough in the present situation.

Cotton cultivation, which used to use free labour, needs the development of harvesting machinery suitable for each grade of cotton.

The present machinery destroys the soil structure by its heaviness, its efficiency is low, and breakdowns are frequent. Drip irrigation systems should be developed where possible. A joint venture with the Israelis has proved at their pilot plot in Uzbekistan that the water consumption per unit of end product can be reduced by a factor of five. It is also true that the technology to save the Aral Sea is available. The biotechnological use of an anti-infiltration screen, invented in the 1950s by local scientists, could reduce water consumption by a factor of 10–100. The technology to deal with the Central Asian grey soils, which restrict germination, has also been proposed. More important is the development of labour-intensive industrial production facilities using local raw materials, as well as the expansion of a network of agro-industries, including warehouses, cold-storage facilities, canning and packaging enterprises, and transportation.

A spirit of self-help

What is necessary, above all, is huge investment and the complete reform of the social system in order to preserve the Aral Sea and its surroundings and to regenerate the Aral ecosystem, which includes humans. This is an urgent task for the present generation, but will also be a task for future generations. International cooperation and foreign investment will certainly be necessary, but what is more necessary is a spirit of self-help. Central Asia creates its own wealth and must decide how to apportion it. Central Asia itself needs to adopt new technologies and new institutions. Without a major shift in production and consumption habits at all levels, and a move from an emphasis on disposability and waste to one on re-use and recycling, there can be no solution either to this specific problem or to the economic crisis facing Central Asia. Such a movement, however, is very weak at present. A question remains: even if the international community comes up with billions of dollars, it is uncertain whether Central Asian leaders will want to borrow money for a scheme that generates no wealth. All aid from the international community may otherwise be wasted. The reason for the destructive irrigated agriculture in the first place was on the one hand a lack of concern for its effects either on the natural environment or on human life, and on the other hand the nature of the political and social structure, which required subsidies from Moscow. That structure still exists in Central Asia, i.e. to get money (e.g. subsidies) from London or Washington, D.C.

Recommendations

Preserving the cultural heritage of Central Asia

Why Kenesari saved Aristan
There is a story in a modern Kazakh novel by Iliyas Esenberlin (1969) about Sultan Kenesari, who lived in the first half of the nineteenth century (1802–1847) just before the completion of the Kazakh annexation to Russia in the 1860s. He tried to establish a Kazakh khanate independent of Russia. One day his followers captured an esteemed Kazakh folk-poet, Aristan, from the Atighay Kazakh clan (belonging to the Middle Horde). Aristan, however, was greedy for money and he received a great for deal helping the Russians to get a map of the Kazakh plains and to identify the location and movement of Kazakh tribes. Aristan had amassed considerable wealth by the time he was captured. When he was taken to Kenesari, he kissed Kenesari's boots and begged him not to kill him. Kenesari tried to hold back his anger and turned pale. He said:

The man who sells his nation is like an infected horse. In order to save other horses, there should not be any mercy for that infected horse. There is only one sentence – death! Although it sounds cruel, the sentence is just.

The followers of Kenesari remained silent. They did not react to Kenesari's decision. Aristan begged Kenesari to allow him to speak for the last time. When Kenesari agreed, Aristan sang a song:

O brother Kenesari, if you like me, I am your dear friend,
Even if you hate me, I'm one of your Alash [Kazakh nation].
I'm the son of Atighay Qarauli,
Who gave your father six wives.

[Keneke, jaqsï körseng qarashïngmïn,
Jek körseng de özîngnîng alashïngmïn,
Atanga altï qatïn alïp bergen
Atïghay Qarauïlding balasïmïn.]

Hearing these lines, Kenesari forgave this greedy poet. Then Kenesari's followers immediately applauded him for his correct decision about Aristan. The reason Kenesari forgave the poet was not because Aristan reminded him that he was an old friend, or because the poet was his kinsman. Aristan was a poet who knew thousands of Kazakh folk tales, epics, and songs. Killing him was equivalent to destroying a rich source of Kazakh culture and identity. Therefore, Kenesari's followers did not react when he sentenced the poet to die, but applauded his decision to free him.

Though this story reminds us of the wisdom and justness of the leaders of the Kazakh as free and independent adventurers, it draws attention to the preservation of the cultural heritage of Central Asia while emphasizing group consciousness.

The difficult situation in Central Asia

Scientists and young researchers are now in a difficult position in Central Asia. If they speak a foreign language and are asked to act as an interpreter, they can earn as much money in one day as their monthly salary. If they can arrange a deal with a foreign business, they may well be tempted to quit academic work. What does this mean? It means that the accumulated scientific legacy will rapidly disappear. Young graduates will not seek a career in the academic world, and the future of Central Asia will not be based on the sound development of society. Once science and culture have disappeared, it will take a very long time to regenerate them.

As for the Aral Sea problem, the main concern is whether the partners in any international cooperative action in Central Asia can afford to establish an effective institution there. The political structure is not stable because the transitional economy is deteriorating. A more powerful and reliable group would be the researchers in each country's research institutes. Science needs a common logic and common values. We should take notice of the researchers' talent and ability, and, more important, foster exchanges with researchers in foreign countries who have the capability to deal with the environmental and other problems that they face.

Coordinating Central Asia research

Research in Central Asia is carried out by three groups: national academies of sciences, institutes of higher learning, and industrial research institutes and centres. The national academies of sciences of Central Asia are the most prestigious centres of scientific research, to the extent that almost all leaders of each country are full members of their academy. The national academy, though fully retaining its independence, cooperates with the government in formulating plans for scientific research and development. The academy is a state agency whose main functions are to organize scientific management and to supervise theoretical research in the natural and social sciences being conducted in all the country's research centres. It also determines the main directions of this research and coordinates it countrywide.

Among the academy's activities are the training of research personnel, the strengthening of ties between science and education, and the introduction of the latest knowledge and discoveries into the curricula and research programmes of higher education institutions. The broad cornerstone of an academy's activities is to blend the development of fundamental and applied research and to strengthen relations between science and the needs of the economy.

It seems clear that we need a carefully developed comprehensive research project for the regeneration of the environment of Central Asia, which should have an international level of significance and be implemented in close cooperation with colleagues from abroad. And it is the national academies of sciences of each republic that possess sufficiently high and versatile scientific potential to produce such a project. Their academies have great experience in the study of natural resources, the environment, and ecology – suffice it to say that a score of academic institutes deals directly with the research problems of the environment and nature.

The establishment of an international research centre

Researchers from Kyoto University in Japan and the Kazakh National Academy of Sciences propose to establish an International Centre for Central Asian Ecology in Central Asia. Its first aim is to undertake research on such global environmental problems as desertification, climate aridization, and radioactive pollution. A second goal is to identify and adapt new technologies and new institutions to Central Asian countries. This International Centre will welcome talented scientists in various fields from abroad as well as supporting (both morally and financially) scientists from Central Asia. The International Centre project proposes to integrate the resources of various scientific specialties on an interdisciplinary basis in order to offer solutions to the major environmental problems of the contemporary world. To achieve this will require a concentration of scientific expertise at an international level, and soundly based cooperation between the academic and industrial sectors. I hope that the international community will agree to this idea and help Central Asia achieve sound development.

References

Alekperov, I. I. 1980. "Current problems of the industrial hygiene of cotton-growers." *Gig. Santi.* 45(10), pp. 38–40.

Carlisle, D. S. 1986. "The Uzbek power elite: Politburo and Secretariat (1938–83)." *Central Asian Survey* 5(3/4), pp. 91–132.

Davydov, M. M. 1949. "The Ob' will enter the Caspian: The Yenisey–Ob'–Aral–Caspian water connection and energy problem." *Sibirskiye ogni*, no. 2, pp. 102–110.

Esenberlin, I. 1969. *Kahar, tarikhi roman* [Anger. A historical story]. Alma-Ata: Dzhazushi.

Izahara, T. 1990. "Raw cotton of the USSR." *Spinning Monthly Report*, June, pp. 32–50 (in Japanese).

Izumi, S. 1960. "The present state of the textile industry of the USSR." *Japan Spinning Monthly* 166, pp. 2–22 (in Japanese).

Juurokuhara, T. 1985. "The present cotton situation of the USSR – the slump in the cotton harvest." *Spinning Monthly Report*, September, pp. 50–56 (in Japanese).

Khalikov, P. K. 1990. "The level of chromosome mutations in the bone marrow cells of wild mice trapped in an area of intensive pesticide use." *Tsitol. Genet.* 24, ISS 5, pp. 10–13.

Khalmetov, R. K. and L. M. Beketova. 1993. "Health status of children and adolescents in the main cotton growing region of Central Asia." *Vestn. Ross. Akad. Med. Nauk*, ISS 6, pp. 43–46.

Khamdamov, K. A. 1976. "Tonographic examinations of the eye in children exposed to effects of pesticides applied agriculturally in some areas of Uzbekistan." *Oftalmol. Zh.* 31(3), p. 226.

Sadikova, S. S. et al. 1990. "Indicators of iron metabolism and cellular immunity in healthy children and in those with iron deficiency anemia in relation to ecological conditions." *Pediatriia*, ISS 8, pp. 41–44.

Sharmanov, T. S. 1989. "Nutrition and health in relation to ecology." *Vestn. Akad. Med. Nauk SSSR*, pp. 27–30.

Tishkov, V. A. 1991. "The Soviet Empire before and after Perestroika." *Theory and Society* 20(5), pp. 603–629.

Zak, P. I. R. and T. S. Ergashev. 1980. "Experimental study of the effect of pesticide Butifos on female gonads." *Med. Zh. Uzb.* 2, pp. 48–50.

Zakhidov, S. T. et al. 1993. "The cytogenetic monitoring of the southern Aral Sea area. An evaluation of the genotoxic activity of the water." *Izv. Akad. Nauk Ser. Biol.*, ISS 1, pp. 95–101.

6

Satellite image maps of the Aral Sea and Central Asia

Toshibumi Sakata

The Syrdarya, which runs through the northern base of the Tien Shan mountains, travels 3,000 kilometres to the Aral Sea. The Amudarya, which starts from the Kunlun mountains and runs north-west through the Pamir Heights into the Aral Sea at its south shore, has a river course of approximately 1,500 kilometres.

The Aral Sea, sitting close to and uphill from the Caspian Sea, has had a very interesting history of change. In ancient times, the Aral Sea presented a completely different landscape, either having been a part of the greater Caspian Sea or not having existed at all. During the Stone Age and the Bronze Age, there once existed a lake between the Caspian Sea and the Aral Sea. Today the Amudarya runs straight to the north, but it used to run to the west. The area south of the Aral Sea had been exposed for a long time to the shifting stream of the river, leading to the expansion of rich soil suitable for agriculture. People came and lived there, forming villages. Agriculture along the Amudarya had become prosperous, and a civilization developed in the Khorezm District. The Syrdarya runs into the Aral Sea on its eastern shore. Agriculture also developed along its banks. From the sixth century on, the irrigation system had expanded the cultivated area and promoted activities based on economic motivation, thus giving birth to some strong kingdoms. The Silk Road became popular

Fig. 6.1 **The change in the level of the Aral Sea: The shaded area represents shrinkage between 1986 and 1993 (Note: not to scale)**

and prosperous, and the region had become the base through which East–West trade was promoted and carried out.

Today this region has a great stretch of agricultural land that straddles the banks of the Amudarya, presenting a view from a satellite as if it were a huge elongated oasis in the middle of a desert. As a result of the Ground Truth Survey carried out in 1994, we have found that the land is good for agriculture if water is made available. For millennia, people have converted desert landscapes into agricultural land through irrigation. However, because of high evapotranspiration, these lands became salinized. In order to flush out those salts from the soil, drainage channels have had to be constructed, but these are quite inadequate at present. Generally speaking, the rise and fall of ancient kingdoms in this region depended to a great extent on control of water sources and courses. Since the 1960s, enormous

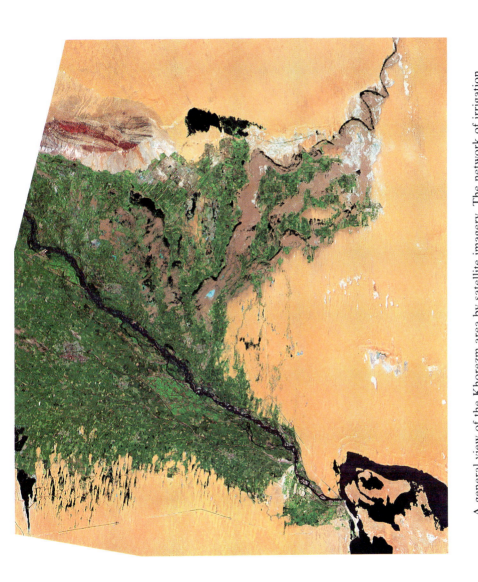

A general view of the Khorezm area by satellite imagery. The network of irrigation canals and the salinization of the surface soils are easily visible (Source: Landsat TM, 2/9/1987)

The Aral and Caspian basins (Source: Landsat TM, 1990, composed by TRIC, Tokai University Research and Information Centre)

The shrinking of the Aral Sea. Left: Aral Sea in 1986. Right: Aral Sea in 1993. The growth of the inland island and the degradation of the coast are easily visible (Sources: left – National Oceanic and Atmospheric Administration [NOAA], 4/9/1980; right – NOAA, 9/7/1993)

Satellite image map of Central Asia (Source: Landsat thematic mapper [TM], 1990, composed by TRIC, Tokai University Research and Information Centre)

efforts by the former Soviet regime to develop cotton fields along the Amudarya and Syrdarya basins have produced large quantities of cotton but also severe degradation of the land, mainly salinization. Furthermore, the construction of many irrigation canals has decreased the influx of water to the Aral Sea.

The Aral Sea of today presents a miserable picture, having lost almost half of its area of the 1960s. According to the analysis of data obtained by satellite, the Aral Sea could disappear some time in the twenty-first century.

7

Voices from the region

A word on Aral

O. Abdirakhmanov

I live in the centre of the Aral region's environmental catastrophe. My people – the people of Karakalpakstan – have no other Mother-land than the Aral region; 1.3 million people now live in the Kar-akalpak Republic. More than 10 million people now live in the ecological disaster zone of the Aral Sea region, as was pointed out in a summary document of a meeting of presidents of Central Asian republics on 3 March 1995. The Aral today is not just a local disaster.

Residents of the Aral region welcome the words of Uzbekistan's President Islam Karimov and Kazakhstan's President Nursultan Nazarbayev, who constantly draw attention to this global problem. As a result of their initiative, the Aral problem has become an integral part of the state politics of the five newly independent states.

The scope of the Aral disaster can be illustrated with the following statistics:

- of the initial surface area of the Aral Sea itself – 66,458 km^2 – slightly more than half remained in the early 1990s;
- of the former volume of water – 1,022 km^3 – only about one-third remained;
- the salt content of the water increased from 10 ppm to 31 ppm;
- the temperature change during the summer months has increased by 2 degrees;
- each hectare of land in the Aral disaster region has 500–700 kg of salt dust that has fallen on it as a result of more frequent and severe dust storms on the newly exposed Aral seabed.

(These data were provided by the Karakalpak Department of the Uzbekistan Academy of Sciences.)

At present over 90 per cent of Karakalpak women of child-bearing age suffer from anaemia and/or low blood pressure. The average infant mortality rate in January and February 1995 was 46 per 1,000 infants under the age of one year. Average life expectancy has been constantly falling.

The drying out of the Aral Sea has taken place in the course of only one human generation, i.e. during a 25-year period, and that cannot but be reflected in both the physical and the spiritual worlds of its people. The rate of population growth has stayed the same, but this is the result of the higher than average birth-rate, and there are ghost "*auls*," or villages, deserted by the population. For example, the village of Ourga had more than 10,000 people living there in 1960, but within a period of five to six years there was not a single person left in the village. All of them had been made to move to the more welcoming (from an environmental standpoint) Kungrad Region. Only a few people knew about this. Back in 1965, when a Communist Party Central Committee Decree was issued on land use and on establishing the USSR Ministry for Water (Minvodhoz), it was impossible to discuss it. The policies for the development of new areas and for changing the direction of flow of rivers were the guiding principle for the state industrial and agricultural systems in the period of totalitarian rule. And at the time people believed in a bright future. When that "bright future" dissolved with the disintegration of the USSR, the indigenous people of the Aral region seemed to have no hope left concerning the Sea's preservation or a better future. Some people had the means to move to prosperous places. Today, the notion of "environmental refugees" appears in the media. Those who had nowhere else to go remained in the land of their ancestors.

Now, however, the people of the Aral region can begin to hope for rescue, thanks to the increase in activity in international circles, due in large measure to the United Nations and especially to the support from international organizations in the form of humanitarian assistance. We are grateful for their help and, together with them, we have come to realize that it is not necessary for us to live the life of a beggar in the world community. As well as humanitarian help, we need investment in our local industries. Today, there are only six joint enterprises in Karakalpakstan, of which only two are in operation, both of them small scale. We need to develop many more such enterprises.

Our oversights are probably as much to blame for this situation, the oversights of activists in the cultural sphere such as writers, journalists, and film-makers. It was perhaps our attempts to draw attention to the rapidly increasing scale of the Aral region's ecological catastrophe that frightened the international community, especially businessmen. This may explain why bigger enterprises are being established far from the Aral region.

Yes, we in Central Asia in general, and in the Karakalpak Republic in particular, have lived at some distance from world civilization. Yes, we have remained in an environmental disaster zone with a backward economy. Yes, our comprehension of the world at large has increased. Yes, we have new state borders following independence. But, we do live in a common world after all, and concern about the Aral ecological disaster zone has been broadening. The appearance of the newly created Aralkum (Aral desert), together with the ancient great deserts of Central Asia – Karakum, Kyzylkum, and Ourst Ourt – could have dangerous regional if not international consequences.

I would like to suggest the following:

1. that all the states of the region set free the region's two great rivers, the Amudarya and the Syrdarya, and readjust their agricultural activities in order to save water resources; it is necessary in planning water consumption to take into consideration the possible needs of the Aral Sea and its surrounding areas;

2. the cooperation of regional states' activities in solving the ecological, economic, and legal problems of the Aral ecological disaster zone, relying when necessary on the help of independent experts from the United Nations and other governmental and nongovernmental organizations.

The role of academic research in solving the ecological problems of the Aral Sea region

U. M. Sultangazin

I will discuss three key ecological problems for the Aral Sea basin:
1. the rationalization of water use,
2. the need to improve water quality,
3. the need to protect and re-create valuable landscapes and ecosystems.

I will show through these examples how wide-ranging data systems and extensive academic research can play an important role in solving these problems.

The National Academy of Sciences of Kazakhstan has been working on the development of a complex programme for the improvement of the ecological situation in the territory of Kazakhstan. In this programme, most attention is centred on the ecological crisis in the Aral and Caspian Sea regions and the nuclear testing site at Semipalatinsk in Kazakhstan, as is introduced by Tsukatani and Sultangazin (1996). About 20 research institutions of the Kazakhstan Academy of Sciences have been involved in the development of this programme. I would like to concentrate on the most significant aspects of this programme.

The rationalization of water use

The first problem is the rationalization of water use based on the comprehensive analysis of regional social and ecological factors. Unfortunately, during the Soviet period, economic decisions were often made without taking into consideration the importance of protecting the environment and the social and economic welfare of the regions involved. For example, a root cause of the "Aral Sea Problem" was the short-sighted economic view of those involved in the development and management of extensive irrigation projects. Driven by the potential for high profit, the environmental consequences of irrigation development were often ignored. This situation still exists in some of the Central Asian republics situated in the upper regions of the Syrdarya watershed. The task of the scientists is to reveal the underlying processes of agricultural and economic development and its impacts and to give qualitative or quantitative forecasts of the consequences of large projects.

The five countries of Central Asia have adopted a plan to solve the ecological problems of the Aral Sea and its adjacent regions. In order to realize this plan it is necessary first of all to determine the optimal distribution of water resources among industries. For this task, we will require information on the economic framework of the republics, the priorities of various industries, population projections, regional geographical information systems (GIS), and watershed management data. We will then be able to use some systems analysis methods to address the problem of the optimal distribution of water resources. Such an approach was introduced in the paper by Sultangazin and Tsukatani (1995), which deals with the distribution of water resources in the Syrdarya basin.

The information system for environmental control comprises three levels: first, monitoring and processing; second, modelling of the environment–economic system; third, environmental control. The scheme for the optimal control of industries in the Syrdarya basin takes into consideration the ecological interests of the Aral Sea. The main constraint is the request for a minimum volume of inflow to the Aral Sea. Other constraints are imposed by the level of technology available to the agricultural sector.

The need to improve water quality

The second problem is how to improve water quality by means of sewage treatment and disposal, and the limitation of waste discharges and of mineral fertilizer use. The uncontrolled use of mineral fertilizers and pesticides has a negative impact on the environment and especially on human health. In the growing season, pollution of Syrdarya's waters by pesticides reaches 12 MPC (maximum permissible concentration); for nitrates it amounts to 46 MPC. Mineralization of water in the Syrdarya (previously fresh) reached 3g/litre, which is 10 times the recommended health standard.

In view of these conditions, the evaluation and control of environmental quality and economic activities in this area should be included in the emergency programmes of the region's policy makers. It has become important to determine priorities for regional environmental policies and to reform the structure of agriculture. Environmental systems are generally considered as multi-objective systems. Optimal standards for environmental quality and economic activities include many conflicting goals. In Sultangazin and Tsukatani (1995) some mathematical models were constructed for the evaluation and management of regional environmental systems. Waste disposal planning is defined at two levels in our models.

The need to protect and re-create valuable landscapes and ecosystems

The degradation of vegetation is occurring over practically the whole of the Aral Sea basin. This is primarily caused by the salinization of soils, resulting from irrigation and salt-dust storms. The number of salt-dust storms has increased with alarming frequency. At present the area of dried seabed is 36,000 km^2 and it is located mostly along the eastern part of the Sea. Every year about 150,000 metric tons of dust and salt are lifted into the atmosphere. If we don't stop this process in future, then the active desertification of adjacent territories and the merging of the newly created Aral desert (the Aralkum) with the Karakum and other deserts in the region may lead to the creation of a new desert of Saharan proportions at the centre of the Euro-Asian continent, which can have only negative consequences. Therefore, first of all it is necessary to create artificial landscape ecosystems in the river deltas and in the dried-up bottom of the Aral Sea. Some results of scientific investigations of phytomelioration prepared by the Academy of Sciences can be used for the creation of artificial ecosystems.

The Kazakh Academy of Sciences has made considerable strides toward solving the problems of natural resource usage in the republic. The research and development activities of a number of institutes during the past 10 years have covered a wide scientific spectrum of the dynamically changing nature of Kazakhstan. For example, the Institute of Hydrology and Hydrophysics is monitoring and investigating the state and environmental condition of groundwater resources in the territory of the republic. The Institute of Geography is investigating the hydro-ecological stability of the Aral and the Caspian Sea basins and is studying the anthropogenic influences on deserts and other geosystems. The Institute of Soil Sciences is investigating the ecological disturbance to soils in southern Kazakhstan (in the valleys of the Syrdarya, Chu, Ili, Talas, Karatal, etc.) and in the region of the Aral Sea, and disturbances on the slopes of Kazakhstan's Tien Shan mountain range. The Institute of Botany is developing phytomeliorative recommendations for the arid areas of the exposed seabed and is conducting investigations into the productivity of pastures and into the biology and ecology of plants in the Aral region. It is also developing maps of plants and of desertification for the territory of Kazakhstan. The Institute of Zoology is studying technogenic factors and agricultural activity that adversely influence the flora and fauna of the republic. At the Institute of Zoology, the state of ecosystems has been analysed, based on surveys of the whole of Kazakhstan. This research has shown that the coastal regions of the Aral and the Caspian Seas are in fact in a state of total degradation.

In spite of rich data obtained by the various institutes of the Academy of Sciences, it is still difficult to obtain an accurate and comprehensive representation of the state of the national environment and the trends of change. Ground-level monitoring is carried out in only a limited number of areas and the extrapolation to other regions is often approximate. Therefore, the application of remote sensing may be very useful for future research and monitoring of environmental changes in Kazakhstan. In applying remote sensing, investigations carried out through test sites by the institutes will be of great importance when deciphering aerospace imagery. The system of environmental monitoring of the territory of Kazakhstan is projected as a set of instruments oriented to resolving existing problems. The system will be developed and new problems will be included in the package. For example, for the atmosphere the following very important problems can be highlighted:
- dust storms in the Aral Sea region, when millions of tons of salt are spread over a large area causing desertification;
- gaseous emissions as a result of accidental breaks in pipes;
- the state of snow cover and icecaps in the Pamir Heights and Tien Shan mountains.
- the transfer of water vapour to Central Asia from other regions.

Concrete tasks for other media will also be developed. Work on complex analyses, using mathematical models, is under way. Information obtained at three levels (space – air – ground) passes through the following stages: data acquisition, transmission, and reception, primary data processing, archiving, and the proposal of solutions to applied problems. The project envisages accomplishing all of the stages. Observations from space will be provided by satellites. Aerial observations are to be carried out on flying laboratories in aircraft. Surface-based observations will be conducted primarily on the testing ground in the Priaralie (the area immediately adjacent to the Aral Sea) and in the neighbouring regions of Almaty.

Some recommendations

First, a geographical information system should be created for the optimal control of the distribution of water resources and of waste disposal, taking into consideration the social and economic interests of the republics in the Aral Sea basin. This can be achieved through the application of the information system described by Sultangazin and Tsukatani (1995), and by mathematical models of the environment and economy.

Secondly, in order to undertake research into global environmental problems of desertification and global warming of the atmosphere and to evaluate the regional environmental situation, it would be valuable to establish an International Centre for Central Asian Ecology in Almaty.

References

Sultangazin, U. M. and T. Tsukatani. 1995. *Modeling of the Kazakhstan Economy and Environment*. Discussion Paper No. 416. Kyoto, Japan: Kyoto University.
Tsukatani, T. and U. M. Sultangazin. 1996. "Current economy and environment of Kazakhstan in 1995." *Japanese Slavic and East European Studies* 16, pp. 95–106.

Iranian strategies in Central Asia

Modjtaba Sadria

In my discussion, I do not use the term "Central Asian republics" as it is usually used in the strict geographical meaning; I include Azerbaijan as a Central Asian republic.

With all its ups and downs, one can divide the interaction between Iran and Central Asia in the modern era into three periods.

The first period began in the second half of the nineteenth century and continued until the Bolshevik Revolution in Russia and the founding of the Pahlavi dynasty in Iran. In this period, the Russian state was continuously expanding its influence in Central Asia, while the inclusion of Iran in the power politics of European powers, including Russia, sometimes went as far as the partition of Iran itself.

During this period, one can say that Iran was acting primarily on a defensive basis, and it did not have many grandiose designs on Central Asia.

The second period began with the Soviet Union's integration into its territory of the whole of Central Asia, sealing off its borders. At that time Iran was entering into a process of modernization in which the creation of a centralized bureaucracy and a national identity occurred in parallel with the weakening of the autonomy of ethnic identities in Iran (i.e. Azeris and Turkmens). During this period of the Pahlavi dynasty, Iran was integrated into the world system mainly as part of first British and then American strategies of containment of the Soviet Union. This essentially sealed off its borders with the Central Asian republics of the Soviet Union. With a few nuances, Iranian attitudes toward the Central Asian republics of the Soviet Union were the same as Iranian attitudes toward the Soviet Union in general. The fear of the rapid growth of military capabilities of the Soviet Union after World War II was another factor that accounted for the absence of cross-border contacts. In this second period, Iran did not have its own Central Asian strategy, although it sometimes had its own Soviet policy. Basically, its position and its role were determined through its integration into the Western political and military strategies regarding the Soviet Union.

The third period started with the foundation of the Islamic republic in Iran. In a simplified way, one can further divide relations between Iran and Central Asia since the birth of the Islamic republic into two periods. The first period was from 1979 to 1988, during which the new republic was confronted with the task of developing the institutions it dealt with in the Iran–Iraq war which, one can argue, had contradictory impacts on the new republic. On the one hand, a long and costly eight-year war accelerated, according to some points of view, the creation and consolidation of new institutions for the Islamic republic. On the other hand, besides its rhetoric, the war had very pragmatic managerial requirements. Ideologies and beliefs can influence the way that these managerial and pragmatic tasks are viewed but cannot replace them. Fighting the war brought to the attention of the new leaders in a more urgent way the necessity of taking into consideration the daily tasks of the state while deepening their awareness of world-scale power relationships as well as geo-strategic considerations.

Fighting the war under multilateral pressures from Western powers, and with access to limited resources, taught the leaders of the Islamic republic to give much more weight to the importance of South–South trade relations. One could say that this element was under consideration by some of the Islamic republic's planners, but the realities of the war and the context in which it was being carried out gave the new state a more realistic view of international relations. Besides the acceptance in principle of the necessity of strengthening South–South relations, there was a practical need to find whatever would make for broader interaction. One can say, paradoxically, that the war with Iraq activated a process of understanding the capacities that Southern countries can optimize in South–South relationships. By the end of the Iran–Iraq war, Gorbachev's *perestroika* was already in crisis. Very soon thereafter, the disintegration of the Soviet Union took place. For the first time in the modern era, an independent Iranian state found itself with political, economic, and cultural options toward the Central Asian republics, which had become politically independent entities both unexpectedly and rapidly.

It is necessary to analyse Iran's misunderstandings and wrong political choices since 1989 in relation to the Central Asian republics. What seems to be more important, though, is not only identifying those wrong political choices, but rather to see the growing trends coming out of Iran. These growing trends can be characterized as follows: consciousness by Iranian decision makers of the complexities of the reality in the Central Asian republics – their approach has become much more nuanced, and much more tempered; consciousness that the outcome of political processes in the Central Asian republics is primarily the result of the activities of political forces within those countries; awareness that the Iranian state must interact primarily with its counterparts, i.e. each state in Central Asia, and that these interactions can last only if mutual benefits derive from them (part of which involves Iran playing a stabilizing role); recognition that the quality of the bilateral relations with each of the republics will create the foundation of Iran's interactions with the whole of Central Asia; acknowledgement that the Iranian presence in Central Asia does not have to be exclusive – other countries with historical relations and affinities towards Central Asia can be present along with Iran. The Economic Cooperation Organization (ECO), which brings together Turkey and Pakistan with Iran for broader regional interactions with the Central Asian republics, is the result from the Iranian perspective of the synthesis of these points.

But Iran, like Turkey, has other frameworks besides the ECO for interaction with the Central Asian republics. The border between Iran and Turkmenistan and the border between Iran and Azerbaijan create the basis for bilateral relations. As important is the fact that countries bordering the Caspian Sea share a natural geographical framework for interactions between Iran and most of the Central Asian republics. Awareness of the massive presence of Russia in the Caspian Sea region constitutes another aspect of Iranian strategies. The accumulated effects of these diversified, but complementary, strategies lead the observer to notice that the growing trend of Iranian strategies towards Central Asia lies increasingly in activating South–South relations among states that face more or less the same kinds of political, economic, and social challenges.

Part III
The Caspian Sea

8

Environmental policy-making for sustainable development of the Caspian Sea area

Genady N. Golubev

Introduction

The Caspian Sea is exceptional by many standards. It is the largest lake in the world. Moreover it is a closed lake with very large variations in its water level because of natural oscillations of the components that make up the water balance. The variations in the water level have had a strong influence on most aspects of economic life. This has been particularly so during the past few decades.

The largest river of Europe, the Volga, plays the principal role in the hydrological regime of the Sea. In addition to water, it also brings, as do other rivers that flow into the Caspian, a considerable amount of pollutants, which influence the aquatic ecosystems including the unique population of the few species of sturgeon. The Sea and its shores are rich with mineral resources, including oil, but prospecting and extraction also require effective environmental management.

The objective of this paper is to analyse the interrelation of the natural and socio-economic issues for the sake of regional sustainable development in a very special region of the world.

Morphometry and the principal hydrological features

The Caspian Sea is so large that it really deserves to be called a Sea. Its area is about 400,000 km², it is 1,200 km long and 170–450 km wide, and its water volume is 80,000 km³. The total length of the shoreline is about 7,000 km. The average depth is 180 m and its maximum depth is 1,025 m. All these data are approximate, because they vary considerably depending on the water level of the Sea.

Morphologically, the Caspian Sea is divided into three main parts, which are more or less equal in area: a very shallow northern part with depths not exceeding 10 m, a middle part with an average depth of 170 m and a maximum depth of 790 m, and the deepest southern part, which has an average depth of 325 m and a maximum depth of 1,025 m (Avakian and Shirokov, 1994). The proportional volumes of the three parts are correspondingly 1/100, 1/3, and 2/3 of the total volume. The salinity of the Caspian Sea water ranges between 0.2 g/litre at the mouth of the Volga to 12–13 g/litre in the central and southern parts.

Because of its relatively small volume and depth, the northern part is the most vulnerable hydrologically and, hence, ecologically and economically. In addition, the shores of the northern part are as flat as its bottom and therefore the shoreline looks very insignificant. The shoreline is very variable, depending on both (a) the longer-term, climate-induced variations in water level of the Sea as a whole and (b) short-term, local wind action. A typical situation would be a rapid increase in sealevel, usually in the cold part of the year, as a result of strong winds, mostly from a southerly direction. In the most catastrophic cases the water level increases by 3.0–4.5 m and, owing to the flat topography, the Sea penetrates far inland, inundating strips 30–50 km wide for a few hundred kilometres along the coast. During the wind-driven waves of 11–13 November 1952 the inundation covered about 17,000 km². In such cases the damage to settlements, roads, oil installations, etc. is very high.

The latest example of wind-driven catastrophic inundation was reported in the press as this chapter was being prepared. During 12–16 March 1995 in Kalmykia, an Autonomous Republic of the Russian Federation situated on the north-western coast of the Caspian Sea, the water level increased up to 3 m. Over 200,000 hectares (2,000 km²) were inundated. Losses of human life were recorded (the exact figure was not given), and 520 houses (home to 3,200 people) were destroyed. About 150,000 sheep were lost.

The Caspian Sea is a closed water body. The main tributary, the Volga, is the largest river of Europe. Its watershed area is 1,360,000 km² or about 40 per cent of the total for the Caspian, but it brings over 80 per cent of the total surface and underground flow to the Sea. From various points of view, the Volga plays a very important role in the state of the Caspian Sea with regard to its water balance, oscillations in its water level, and its chemical and biological make-up. Through these factors the Volga influences the socio-economic development of the Sea and the adjacent territories.

The Volga River basin belongs completely to the Russian Federation. It contains about 40 per cent of Russia's population and is responsible for one-third of both the industrial and agricultural production of Russia. Psychologically, the river is viewed as "Mother Volga," the nation's main river. An integrated, sustainable environmental management for the Caspian Sea is impossible without a proper programme of action for the Volga basin. Such a programme would extend international cooperation on the Caspian deep inside Russia to Moscow.

The water balance and water-level variations

The data on the Sea's water balance vary considerably, depending on the time-period being considered and the incompleteness of knowledge. It is not the objective of this paper to go deeply into these issues. As an illustration, however, average data for 1900–1985 are shown in table 8.1. The mean annual deficit of the water balance – 12 km³ – corresponds to the mean annual drop in water level of 3.1 cm. The average water level for the 1900–1985 period was −27.35 m above sealevel (a.s.l.), or 27.35 m below the ocean level.

Most components of the water balance do not need explanation.

Table 8.1 **The average water balance of the Caspian Sea, 1900–1985**

Component	km³/year
River inflow	+298
Precipitation on the Sea's surface	+74
Evaporation from the Sea's surface	−370
Outflow to the Bay of Kara-Bogaz-Gol	−14
Total	−12

Source: adjusted data from Kosarev and Makarova (1988).

The Kara-Bogaz-Gol is a large bay situated on the eastern side of the Caspian Sea. Because of its elevation, there is a constant flow in one direction, from the Sea to the bay, with subsequent evaporation of water from the bay.

The variations in the components of the Caspian water balance are considerable; this leads to large changes in water level. The main factor in variations in the water balance is changes in river runoff, particularly that of the Volga.

During the twentieth century, the main periods of change in the Caspian Sea's water regime were as follows (Kuksa, 1994):

1900–1929: Relative stability of the water balance. The water level oscillated slightly around 26.2 m below sea-level.

1930–1941: A very large deficit in the water balance of 62 km^3, mainly because of the decrease in river runoff (mostly that of the Volga). The water deficit led to a sharp drop in the water level of 1.8 m.

1942–1977: A modest deficit in the water balance mainly because of a decrease in river runoff. During this period there was a drop in the water level of an additional 1.3 m.

1978–present: A positive water balance. The water level has been increasing from its lowest point of -29.0 m in 1977. By 1994 it had risen to about -26.5 m, an increase in this period of 2.5 m.

For not very clear seasons, researchers in the 1970s and earlier were under the impression that water withdrawals in the Caspian basin, mainly for irrigation and to fill the large, newly constructed water reservoirs, played a decisive role in variations in the water balance. In fact, variations of natural origin explain about 90 per cent of all variations (Golytsyn and Panin, 1989). Water withdrawals in the Sea basin amount to 40–50 km^3/year, about half of which are from the Volga basin. Without human interference, the Sea's level might have been about 1.5 m higher than it is now (Kuksa, 1994).

The continuous, prolonged drop in the level of the Caspian caused a panic that reached its height in the 1970s. A number of long-term water-level projections were published, using different approaches to forecasting. Some were based on analysis of inflow to and evaporation from the Sea. They were not successful, because the behaviour of these factors is close to that of "white noise." Attempts were made to base projections on the index of solar radiation (the so-called Wolf's numbers), but they proved to be very contradictory. Forecasts based on indices of atmospheric circulation also provided unstable results. The only seemingly reasonable basis for projections was the forecast of water withdrawals, and this approach led to the conclusion that the level of the Caspian Sea would continue to fall (Shikloma-nov, 1979). The common opinion that the level of the Caspian Sea would continue to drop had been strongly reinforced by the similar sharp drop in the level of the Aral Sea just a few hundred kilometres to the east of the Caspian Sea.

Very drastic and very costly measures were considered to maintain the level of the Caspian. Projects were proposed to bring large amounts of water from the north (e.g. Siberian rivers) to the south of the country (Golubev and Biswas, 1979, 1985). If they had been carried out, they would have had unforeseen and costly consequences.

In the 1980s, the situation changed completely. The Caspian water level continued to rise. Since all kinds of forecasts had indicated the continuation of a declining sealevel, this can serve as an example of a collective miscalculation by many very good water experts. The sealevel, however, has continued to grow in the 1990s, generating worries for the future, although actual problems of inundation and destruction as well as recent sealevel rises have had a major effect on the economy of locales around the Sea's shore.

The situation of oscillations in the level of the Caspian Sea is typical of closed lakes. It is typical not only from the hydrometeorological point of view, but from the point of view of economic impacts as well. The variations in sealevel cause uncertainty over time in economic activities. The interest groups involved, including governments, have to develop a long-term strategy for the management of the region. Thus, it is important to determine the expected upper and lower extremes with a reasonable probability of occurrence.

The history of variations in the level of the Caspian Sea (Klige, 1992) provides useful insights into this issue. During the period of instrumental observations (fig. 8.1) from 1837 on, the water level varied between −25 m and −29 m a.s.l., with an average of −27 m. From the sixth century B.C. to the present, the sealevel ranged from −20 m to −34 m, a variation of 14 m (fig. 8.2). The average level, however, was the same: −27 m. During the Holocene (the past 10,000–11,000 years), the sealevel ranged from −9 m to −34 m (fig. 8.3), a variation of 25 m. The mean sealevel was −25 m a.s.l.

Fig. 8.1 **Variations in the water level of the Caspian Sea according to instrumental observations, 1837–2000 (Source: Klige, 1992)**

(Note that the curves in these figures are not completely consistent, owing to differences of methodology and measurement.)

The rates of water-level change are also important. The typical rate for pronounced changes is about 150 cm per 10 years; this happened twice in the twentieth century. Over longer periods of time, the typical figure for sharp changes is about 10 m over a period of 1,000 years. If one is to believe the data in figure 8.3, the extreme rate of change is about 14 m over 300 years; or a 14 m increase and then a 14 m drop over 700–800 years. Thus, sharp variations in the level of the Caspian Sea are the most characteristic feature of its regime at time-scales of tens and hundreds of years. Economic development strategies must take this into consideration.

The unsuccessful experiences with forecasting Caspian Sea behaviour indicate that, given the present-day level of scientific understanding, reliable forecasts cannot be expected. One has to plan on the basis of expectations of quasi-cyclical oscillations in sealevel, as has happened in the past. Most researchers believe that in the next

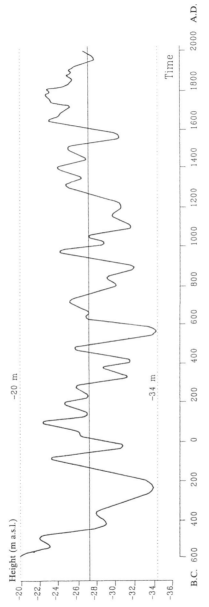

Fig. 8.2 **Variations in the water level of the Caspian Sea during historic time (sixth century B.C. to the present) (Source: Klige, 1992)**

97

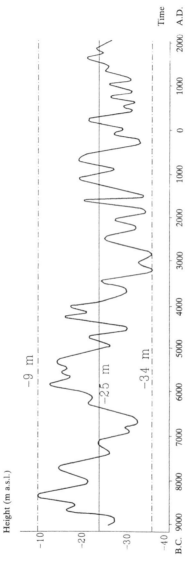

Fig. 8.3   Variations in the water level of the Caspian Sea during the Holocene (Source: Klige, 1992)

decade the sealevel will reach -25 m. In the longer term, variations in sealevel are expected to range between -20 m and -29 m.

During the prolonged drop in sealevel between 1930 and 1977, when it was believed that the trend would continue, economic planning considered the low sealevel. New settlements or roads, ports, oil installations, and so forth were built on the assumption of a sealevel of -28 m. Now, however, with the sealevel approaching -26 m, economic damage in each of the riparian countries has been enormous.

Owing to the relatively rapid rise in sealevel, the Caspian coastline is currently in a state of transition. In general, the change from the retreating phase of the Caspian to the advancing phase has led to a transition from predominantly accumulating processes along the shore to a prevalence of abrasion processes. On formerly accumulating shores, erosion processes have begun and continue in many places. In quite a number of areas erosion has been catastrophic. Cliffs used to be separated from the Sea by a wide beach. Now, the cliffs are subjected to wave action, and the eroded soils have accumulated on the former beaches. Many houses, apartment buildings, hotels, and other structures constructed in the 1930s to 1970s close to the cliffs are now in danger or are in the process of being destroyed. Experience has shown that construction of any kind, except ports, should be at levels above -23 m.

The economic impacts on the Caspian states of the water-level variations

The present situation

On the flat territory of the northern and north-western coast, which belongs to the Russian Federation, even small increments in the water level mean large losses of land. If the water level reaches -25 m, 16,500 km^2 will be lost, of which 10,000 km^2 would be inundated and 6,500 km^2 waterlogged. This land has oil and gas wells, roads, irrigated and other arable land, etc. At -25 m, 114 human settlements would be inundated, with a total population of 100,000. The frequency and magnitude of the floods caused by wind action will increase. The current strategy in the Russian part of the Caspian coast is to plan for a water level between -26 and -25 m, keeping in mind wind-caused floods up to -23 to -22 m. Construction of a protecting dike with a road along the top is envisaged for most of the

north-western coast. In addition, special engineering action is foreseen to protect certain towns and the railway going north–south
along the coast. This railway is the only one leading from the centre
of the country to the south that does not cross the zone of the recent
military conflict and political instability in the northern Caucasus.

Information on damage to the territories of the riparian countries
other than Russia is scanty. The north-eastern shoreline belonging to
Kazakhstan is also extremely flat. Wind-driven waves cause floods,
which are the biggest nuisance. The height of these floods reaches 2.3–
2.8 m, with inundation inland up to 30–40 km (Kuksa, 1994). During
the last quarter of the twentieth century there have been 10 floods
like this. During wind-induced flooding, behind the flooding wave
(that is, towards the Sea) an area of low sealevel is formed, up to 3 m
below the average within a band 10–15 km wide. Western Kazakhstan is rich in oil and gas resources. A sealevel rise and the associated
increase in the frequency of wind-wave inundations are very serious
obstacles to further development of the oil and gas industry.

In Turkmenistan the increase in sealevel has created some problems as well. The most serious situation is around the town of
Cheleken, situated on the peninsula of the same name. During the
days of relatively high sealevels before 1930, Cheleken was an island.
Then, with the drop in sealevel, it became a peninsula. Now, it is
turning once again into an island. The dike that protects the town has
been destroyed by waves and dozens of apartment buildings are
under water, along with two adjacent settlements. Oil and gas pipelines, the main road leading inland, and port installations have been
damaged; drilling rigs and power supply lines are surrounded by
water. Sewage treatment facilities in the area and, hence, the ecology
of the Sea are endangered. In some places sea water has penetrated
inland by 40 km (Kuksa, 1994).

A unique feature on the eastern shore of the Caspian Sea is the
Bay of Kara-Bogaz-Gol, which belongs to Turkmenistan. In 1980 the
area of the Bay was 9,500 km^2. The water level in Kara-Bogaz-Gol is
a few metres below that of the Sea, and there is a constant flux of
water into the bay. At the beginning of the twentieth century, when
the water level was about −26 m, the flux to the bay was about
20 km^3 a year. The bay served as a large evaporation pan. Water
evaporated in the bay, leaving a brine that was very rich in valuable
chemical elements and salts. By 1980, the brine contained 270–290 g
of salt per litre. The total volume of the brine was 20–22 km^3 and its

average depth was 2.1 m. The total amount of dissolved salts was 6 billion metric tons (Bortnik, 1991), supporting a productive chemical industry.

In 1977–1978, however, with the water level close to −29 m, the discharge of water to the bay was only 5–7 km^3. To slow down the drop in the level of the Caspian Sea, a decision was made in 1978 to cut off Kara-Bogaz-Gol from the rest of the Caspian. This was accomplished by March 1980, *after* the sealevel had already begun to increase. The bay stayed completely cut off from the Sea for four and a half years, during which about 50 km^3 of Caspian water had been saved. This corresponded to a 12–14 cm rise in the level of the entire Sea. However, by that time it was no longer needed. By the first half of 1984 the valuable brine had dried up at the surface of the bay and much of it had crystallized and settled on the bay's bottom. A viable chemical industry had died. It was then decided to restore the connection between the bay and the Sea. Now, a new, much smaller brine basin is being formed inside the bay close to the strait. The current status of the chemical industry is not known. The problem, which had been created by the Soviet Union, is now in the hands of the new state of Turkmenistan.

In Iran, the impacts on its flat coastal landscape have also been considerable. Protecting barriers of 8.5 km have been built, and an additional 27 km are needed (Mojtahed-Zadeh, chap. 9 in this volume).

In Azerbaijan, the Lenkoran Lowland is a continuation of the lowlands of Iran. In the town of Lenkoran at least 500 houses have been destroyed and 800 hectares of fertile land have been lost. The protected nature area of Kizil-Agach, a wetland convenient for wintering a great variety of migratory birds, is now almost completely under water.

The need for international cooperation

This brief review of the damage associated with the rise in the level of the Caspian Sea brings us to a very important conclusion: stabilization of the level of the Caspian Sea is in the interests of all countries surrounding the sea. This might provide a basis for international cooperation with regard to a lot of give-and-take issues. Obviously, a total or partial stabilization of the sealevel is beyond human means, but some modest degree of control is possible, as the Kara-Bogaz-Gol experience has demonstrated. Another possibility would be to use the flat territories of the north-eastern Caspian as evaporation pans; they had in fact been working that way before the sealevel dropped in the 1930s.

Theoretically, it is also possible to control the sealevel by regulating water consumption in the basin, mainly in the Volga River basin. However, this would involve a very complex political problem: the Volga and its basin belong to one country, the Russian Federation, while the Caspian Sea belongs to five. Moreover, the portion of the shoreline belonging to Russia is modest. Management of an international lake (or sea) by means of action in a large but national river would not be a trivial diplomatic issue.

Another option would be large water transfers from neighbouring northern basins. About 10 years ago such proposals were sharply (and justly) criticized by the environmental movement. Neither the present political climate nor current levels of science and technology are yet good enough to reconsider such projects.

Developing a common strategy for sustainable economic activity on the Caspian Sea (and its shores) under conditions of drastic changes in the sealevel is a very good subject for negotiation and cooperation. It is not, however, a trivial subject; international cooperation is not just desirable but absolutely necessary.

Other development issues requiring international cooperation

Other important development issues for the Caspian Sea require international cooperation. Two are briefly mentioned here: the management of marine biological resources and the management of mineral resources in the seabed, primarily oil and gas.

Marine biological resources

The northern part of the Caspian Sea is of very high biological productivity. Primary biological production amounts to 23 million metric tons a year. In addition, the rivers (primarily the Volga) carry about 20 million tons of organic matter a year from the basin (Katunin et al., 1990, cited in Kuksa, 1994). Therefore, the importance of the Caspian Sea for fisheries is high. During 1976–1981, the average annual fish catch, mostly from the northern Caspian, was about 400,000 tons. The Caspian is a unique body of water containing about 90 per cent of the world population of sturgeon species. Unfortunately, the share of sturgeon in the total catch is declining, being about half what it was during the first decade of the twentieth century. The main causes are the construction of dams on rivers, which cut off the main spawning grounds, increased water pollution, and the reduction of streamflow due to withdrawals for irrigation. Sustainable maintenance of the unique Caspian ecosystem is clearly one of the priority actions to be pursued through cooperation by all five Caspian nations.

Mineral resources

One of the very first oil fields to be exploited is around Baku, the largest Caspian city and the capital of Azerbaijan. Today, oil and gas fields are everywhere along the shores of the Sea. The fields extend into the Sea and there is considerable experience, mainly close to Baku, in extracting oil from the Sea's bottom.

After the collapse of the Soviet Union a problem emerged of how to use natural resources from the bottom of a large international lake (or sea). No less serious a problem is the proper environmental management of the Sea in the course of oil and gas prospecting and extraction from the seabed. One of the primary legal issues is to define what the Caspian is – a sea or a lake, because they can be legally treated differently, depending on the definition.

The list of issues related to the sustainable development of the Caspian Sea and its coastline addressed here has not been exhaustive. A first step toward the international cooperation process should be to define the priorities of interest of each of the riparian Caspian countries.

Conclusions

Nature must be respected. This is particularly true of the Caspian Sea region. It is a special case of closely integrated natural, political, environmental, social, and economic issues. It is in the interests of all branches of the economy to learn how to move on along the road of sustainable development, given the very large variations in the sea-level. This will be impossible, however, without effective international cooperation. Broadly speaking, effective management of the Caspian Sea and its resources cannot be achieved without concerted action by all five riparian countries. Only a holistic approach at the international level can make economic development of the region truly sustainable.

Acknowledgement

The author expresses his very deep appreciation to Prof. Rudolf K. Klige for providing the graphs of the variations in the level of the Caspian Sea (figs. 8.1, 8.2, and 8.3).

References

Avakian, A. B. and V. M. Shirokov. 1994. *Rational Use and Protection of Water Resources*. Ekaterinburg: Publ. House "Victor" (in Russian).

Bortnik, V. N. 1991. "The water balance of the Bay of Kara-Bogaz-Gol under natural and controlled conditions." *Trudy GOIN*, no. 183, pp. 3–18 (in Russian).

Golubev, G. N. and A. K. Biswas (eds.). 1979. *Interregional Water Transfer: Projects and Problems*. Oxford: Pergamon Press.

———— 1985. *Large-Scale Water Transfers: Emerging Environmental and Social Experiences*. Oxford: Tycooly Publishing, for UNEP.

Golytsyn, G. S. and G. N. Panin. 1989. "Once more on the water level changes of the Caspian Sea." *Vestnik Akademii Nauk SSSR*, no. 9, pp. 59–63 (in Russian).

Katunin, D. N., A. G. Ardabieva, L. N. Dubovskaya, and N. V. Ivanova. 1990. "Primary productivity processes in northern Caspian under anthropogenic impact." Paper presented at the 8th All-Union Conference on Applied Oceanology, Leningrad, 15–19 October (in Russian).

Klige, R. K. 1992. "Changes in the water regime of the Caspian Sea." *GeoJournal*, July, pp. 299–307.

Kosarev, A. N. and R. A. Makarova. 1988. "On the changes in the Caspian Sea water level and the possibility of forecasting it." *Vestnik Mosk. Universiteta, Geographia*, no. 1, pp. 21–26 (in Russian).

Kuksa, V. I. 1994. *Southern Seas (Aral, Caspian, Azov and Black) under Anthropogenic Stress*. St. Petersburg: Hydrometeoizdat (in Russian).

Shiklomanov, I. A. 1979. *Anthropogenic Changes in River Run-Off*. Leningrad: Hydrometeoizdat (in Russian).

9

Iranian perspectives on the Caspian Sea and Central Asia

Pirouz Mojtahed-Zadeh

Introduction

The decade of the 1990s began with tremendous changes in the global political system. These profound changes prepared the framework for an entirely new set of geopolitical circumstances for the twenty-first century. From the point of view of political geography, 1991 was an outstanding year, in the sense that it was the year during which two major events occurred that highlighted the rapid rate of change in the global system. The first was the Kuwait crisis, which triggered an almost universal reaction. This, in turn, gave birth to the concept of "international community" to replace the term "free world" in the dying days of the communist bloc. The second event was the collapse of the geostrategic structure of the Warsaw Pact, which not only destroyed former communist states such as the former Soviet Union, Yugoslavia, and Czechoslovakia, but also brought down the bipolar system that had evolved in the wake of World War II. These developments accelerated the speed of the globalization of the interests and aspirations of many nations. This further intensified political and economic competition worldwide.

These political equivalents of a global earthquake shook the global political system, with staggering regional results, especially for the area of our particular concern extending from central Europe to the Pacific Ocean, and in the area known as the Middle East. Regional issues tend to dominate an individual nation's foreign policy considerations and regional interests. This, in turn, is the basis on which the globalization of interests has been gradually developing.

The new geopolitical realities have fundamentally changed the balance of forces in the international community. Global thinkers proposed visions of what they perceived could be a New World Order: (a) a unipolar system with the United States at the top of the pyramid of the global structure playing the role of the "global gendarme," (b) a clash of civilizations, and (c) the beginning of a multipolar economically oriented global system (Mojtahed-Zadeh, 1992). The recent demise of the ideologically oriented bipolar world is evidence of the changing geopolitical structure.

The end of the Cold War was marked by an unprecedented intensification of economic competition among North America, Western Europe, and Pacific Rim countries. The economic successes of the European Union encouraged other economic powers to form regional economic groupings of their own. For example, the United States joined with Canada and Mexico to create the North American Free Trade Agreement. Countries in South-East Asia had already formed the Association of South-East Asian Nations.

The emergence of these regional economic groupings as giants presents a picture of how the changing world order is shaping up on the brink of the twenty-first century. Although the "paper" successor to the Soviet Union, the Commonwealth of Independent States (CIS), with both Slavic and Islamic members, may not survive in its present form, the possibility exists that increased rivalries with, as well as encouragement from, other geostrategic regions will result in the formation of a more realistic grouping between Russia and, for example, some of the nations of Eastern Europe. However, today most East European nations strive to join NATO and the European Union. In Asia, China's expanding economy, together with its reunification with Hong Kong in 1997 and a wider economic grouping with other countries in the region, will result in the formation of yet another regional economic giant.

Other regional economic arrangements will be the subject of change and modification in terms of goals, structure, and geographical scope. The Economic Cooperation Organization (ECO) is one such arrangement. This grouping includes Iran, Turkey, Pakistan, Azerbaijan, Kazakhstan, Turkmenistan, Uzbekistan, Tajikistan, Kyrgyzstan, and

Afghanistan. As a regional organization, it has never functioned seriously and needs fundamental changes in terms of its structural shape and its regional and global aspirations before being able to function in the new geopolitical environment. A news report in 1995 noted that "ECO officials boast of the region's potential, 300 million people with rich natural resources. But it will be a huge task to make it anything like a real common market" (*The Economist*, 2 December 1991, p. 42).

In sum, with the demise of communism, ideological rivalries in the global system have been increasingly replaced by economic competition. What was once described as the capitalist economy has become the prevailing global economic system. Increased global exchange – to be further boosted by the World Trade Organization as a successor to the General Agreement on Tariffs and Trade – has undermined many aspects of the economic sovereignty of nation-states.

In the emerging global political system Iran is uniquely situated as a land-bridge connecting two very important regions – the Caspian–Central Asia region and the Persian Gulf region. This geopolitical position has had an immense influence on Iran's global and regional policies as well as on the policies of other powers toward these two regions. Iranian policy makers, however, do not appear to have formulated, as yet, a clearly defined strategy for maximizing the influence of Iran's unique geographical position between two of the most important areas of energy deposits on earth. Iran's evolving strategies, still somewhat vague, have not yet brought home to the international community the message that Iran's territory is geographically and economically the most logical and most sensible route to pipe oil and gas from the Caspian and Central Asian regions to the high seas by way of the Persian Gulf and the Gulf of Oman. This is especially true if one considers the export of oil to Japan and to other major oil consumers in the Far East. Full realization of this position is bound to lead to a substantial modification of Iran's political outlook as well as the modification of the reactions of others in response to Iranian policies.

Iran's new geostrategic position has led it to identify two major regions of direct interest: one to the north and one to the south. This paper presents an overview of Iran's northern geopolitical interests in the Caucasus, the Caspian Sea region, and Central Asia. It also includes a brief discussion of Iran's eastern hydropolitics: the case of Lake Hamun and the Hirmand River on the southern edge of Central Asia.

Iran's northern geopolitical interests

Iran's northern geopolitical interests are complex but can be defined in terms of their geographical dimensions. Three regions of direct interest to Iran are the Caucasus, the Caspian Sea, and Central Asia.

The Caucasus

The Caucasus is a region of mixed Moslem and Christian nations with limited economic resources. Establishing strong ties with Georgia, Armenia, Azerbaijan, and others in this region is highly significant for Iran. The Caucasus does not, however, have top priority in Iran's geopolitical interests, except when provoked by its traditional rivalries with Turkey and Russia. Also, the dual nature (from the Iranian point of view) of Azerbaijan's geographical position in this region commands Iran's special attention, because (a) the Republic of Azerbaijan is the geographical continuation of Iran's Azerbaijan provinces, which represents a major geostrategic sensitivity for Iran; and (b) the Republic of Azerbaijan is a major oil-exporting country of the Caspian Sea region with good prospects for assisting Iran in its oil activities in this region.

The Caspian Sea

Iran is one of five states that border on the Caspian Sea and, therefore, has substantial interests in that region. The four other Caspian coastal states are Kazakhstan, Azerbaijan, Russia, and Turkmenistan (fig. 9.1).

The Caspian Sea is highly significant for Iran from an economic point of view. An economic cooperation arrangement among the riparian nations could prove to be very beneficial to them all. It could also assure a significant position for such a regional arrangement in the world's changing international power structures. With gas reserves of 57.1 trillion m^3, this region ranks first in the world, and, with 59.2 billion barrels of oil reserves, it ranks as the world's third most important oil region. At least four regional economic and environmental problems require attention.

Water pollution
Water pollution caused by the excessive concentration of oil products and phenols in the northern (Russian) and eastern (Turkmenistan)

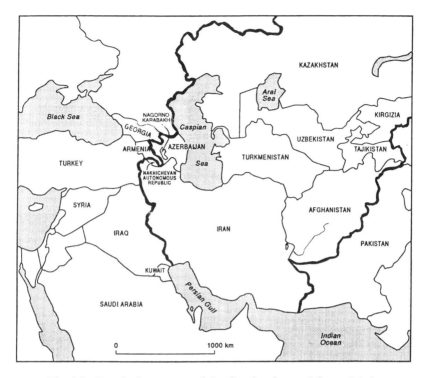

Fig. 9.1　**Iran in the context of the Caspian Sea and Central Asia**

coastal areas of the Caspian exceeds the maximum allowable level by four to six times; along its western coast (Azerbaijan) this pollution level is 12 to 16 times higher than allowable (Soviet Business Intelligence Bureau, 1993, p. 47).

The rise in the level of the Caspian Sea
The rapid rise in the level of the Caspian Sea over the past two decades has caused considerable damage to the coastal areas of all five riparian states. In Mazandaran Province, one of three Iranian provinces bordering the Sea, 9.9 billion Iranian rials (US$1 = Rls70) has been spent constructing 8.5 km of barriers along the coasts of Bándar Turkmen, Nowshahr, Ramsar, and Tonekabon. An additional 27 km still need to be constructed in the same province (*Ettelaat International*, 20 September 1995, quoting reports from the Governorate General of Mazandaran).

A 1947 Iranian study (Barimani, 1947, pp. 78–90) suggests that the rise in the level of the Caspian Sea is a periodic phenomenon recur-

109

ring a few times a century (about every 30–35 years), usually after a few consecutive wet winters. This study provides evidence from early Islamic geographers (such as Masudi), which, although anecdotal, noted great historical variations in the water level of the Caspian Sea. Because of these and more recent observations (see chap. 8 in this volume), there has been considerable research interest among the riparian states in the causes and the ecological and societal impacts of the rise in the level of the Caspian Sea.

The Caspian legal regime

In the past the Caspian Sea was bordered by only two riparian states: Iran and the Soviet Union. Several agreements between the two states governed the Sea's maritime legal regime. As a result of the breakup of the former Soviet Union, five independent countries now border the Sea.

In 1992 the Iranians embarked on the creation of the Council of Caspian Sea Countries (CCSC). This council is to include the five states bordering the Sea. Iran has been slow to define its role in the region. It could, however, be able to function as a forum to discuss matters related to the common interests of the riparian states formulating the means and methods such as for defining the legal regime of the Sea. This slow progress can, in part, be attributed to the way in which some riparian states and Western oil companies rushed in to gain concessions, sometimes in disputed offshore areas that were claimed by more than one coastal authority.

An intergovernmental conference, held in the Russian city of Astrakhan on 15 October 1993, with the participation of Russia, Azerbaijan, Turkmenistan, and Kazakhstan, discussed the Russian desire to establish a common position within the CIS that could then be presented to Iran. The Russians argued that the 1921 treaty signed between the former Soviet Union and Iran forms the basis on which the Caspian legal regime can evolve (*NEFTE Compass*, 24 November 1993). This treaty provides for both Iran and the former Soviet Union to have equal rights of free navigation on the Sea. This regime would allow the Sea to be an object of common use by riparian states on an equal basis. However, implementation of this regime would, no doubt, cause considerable economic "damage" to the oil companies that have invested in exploration in the concession areas granted by the Republic of Azerbaijan.

The Republic of Azerbaijan prefers a 10-, 20-, or 40-mile exclusive economic zone offshore of each state (Khodadov, 1995). Western interests favour this argument against the Russian position. The United States supports the Republic of Azerbaijan and the US-led Azeri oil consortium, arguing that delimitation of the Sea is the most logical, equitable, and workable resolution of national rights to the Sea's resources (Race, 1995). Unhappy about the expansion of oil exploration by Azerbaijan and Western companies, Iran and Turkmenistan are gradually moving toward the Russian position (*Daily Salam of Tehran*, 3 July 1995, reporting statements by Iran's Minister of Foreign Affairs in Switzerland). These three states appear to be formulating a common policy *vis-à-vis* the issue of the Caspian Sea's legal regime. In 1995, leading officials of Russia, Iran, and Turkmenistan warned that use of Caspian Sea resources should be considered illegal until such a legal regime had been formulated (*Ettelaat International*, 11 August 1995, quoting Turkmenistan's Minister of Foreign Affairs). The Russians went so far as to declare that exploration of Caspian Sea resources before such a legal regime had been formulated should be considered illegal (*Echo of Iran*, Aug./Sep. 1995, p. 7, reporting statements by the Russian Deputy Minister of Foreign Affairs in Turkey). The Iranians also warned that the unilateral exploitation of the Caspian Sea before the establishment of a legal system could jeopardize cooperation in the Caspian Sea region (*Ettelaat International*, 10 August 1995, reporting statements by the Iranian Minister of Foreign Affairs in Almaty). These legal uncertainties have resulted in noticeable complications in the development of the maritime activities of each state. For instance, the Republic of Azerbaijan has granted various companies oil exploration concessions that extend far to the east into areas considered by the Republic of Turkmenistan to be within its maritime jurisdiction. The riparian states remain engaged in consultations concerning the future legal regime of the Caspian Sea.

The geopolitics of oil pipelines

The issue of exporting oil from the Caspian Sea region to the outside world has attracted great attention. Iran's geographical position between the Caspian Sea and the Persian Gulf provides an outstanding opportunity for oil and gas pipelines to run from the Caspian Sea to the Persian Gulf and the Gulf of Oman. Not only does this geographical location offer the shortest route for oil and gas from the Caspian Sea region to markets in Japan and the Far East, but Iran's 90 years of experience in the oil and gas industries and its existing oil and gas installations, port facilities, refineries, and networks of oil and gas pipelines offer considerable advantages to Caspian oil and gas exporters.

Iran's existing gas pipeline networks are already connected to the Republic of Azerbaijan and they are within a short distance of the Republic of Turkmenistan. A pipeline connecting Kazakhstan and Turkmenistan to this network would be at least four times shorter in length and much cheaper than any of the proposed lines to other outlets such as the Black Sea and the Mediterranean. The alternative networks would, moreover, have to pass through mountainous areas where various ethnic groups are involved in political struggles against one another as well as against national governments in the region. This would reduce the security of the trans-Caucasus line to a minimum.

Iran signed an agreement with Turkmenistan on 30 January 1995, whereby Turkmen oil would at first be transported to Iran overland and later would be piped to the nearby Iranian refineries. It would then be exported to distant world markets through Iran's Persian Gulf ports (*Ettelaat International*, 1 February 1995). In fact, the first consignment of 3,200 tons of Turkmen oil was reported to have been shipped on 1 February 1995 to the northern Iranian port of Bandar Noshahr for onward transit for export (*Ettelaat International*, 23 February 1995). Other companies operating in Central Asia are also reported to be trying to transport crude through Iran to the Persian Gulf.

In a different development, the Republic of Azerbaijan offered to allocate 5 per cent of its share in the Azerbaijan International Oil Consortium (AIOC) to Iran, allowing Iran to participate in the oil activities of Azerbaijan in the Caspian Sea and to facilitate construction of an oil pipeline across Iranian territory to provide access to a Turkish port on the Mediterranean. An official request was made of Iran in that respect after a contract was signed between the Azeri Oil Company and the National Iranian Oil Company (NIOC) on 3 February 1995 (*Ettelaat International*, 6 February 1995). The Azerbaijan Republic's offer to allot to Iran 5 per cent of its share in the AIOC was withdrawn in April 1995 as a result of US pressure. Nevertheless, the republic continued to encourage Iran to participate in other areas of oil activities within the country. Several factors dictate cooperation between Azerbaijan and Iran. For example, apart from ethnic, historical, and religious affinities between the two countries, much of the south-eastern parts of Azerbaijan's offshore oil fields are shared with Iran. This provides Iran with the possibility of exploiting the fields without additional outside participation. In any case, US pressure on Azerbaijan goes against its tradition of cross-border collaboration with Iran. Having benefited for several decades from the hydropolitics of cooperation over the border river Aras, Iran and the Republic of Azerbaijan have developed a considerable capacity for cooperation in various fields. It must have been on this basis that in May 1995 Azerbaijan declared that it was still possible for the crude oil produced by AIOC to be partly exported via Iran to the Persian Gulf.

Iran has suggested the construction of a pipeline network that would connect Caspian–Central Asian oil exporters with the Persian Gulf. One of the projects proposed by Iranian Foreign Ministry officials consists of a gas loop system involving Iran that has the potential of connecting 70 per cent of the world gas reserves of Russia and Iran in the Persian Gulf, supplying both Europe and Asia with adequate gas supplies in the twenty-first century. An important advantage of this proposed network over other projects is that nearly half of this loop is already in existence and operational (Ghorban, 1994, p. 297). This ambitious system would connect the Caspian–Central Asia region with Europe on the one hand, and with India and the Far East on the other.

The Iranian Oil Ministry has presented Turkmenistan with elaborate technical studies (including route maps) for Turkmenistan's proposed US$3 billion, 1,400 km pipeline in order to deliver 15–30 billion m^3 of natural gas annually to Europe by way of Iran and Turkey (*NEFTE Compass*, 28 July 1994). The Iranians have discussed with Turkmen representatives the possibility of developing a 120,000 barrels/day crude oil pipeline to Iranian refineries (*NEFTE Compass*, 14 July 1994). Yet another project for the Turkmen–Iranian oil pipeline to deliver 400,000 barrels/day to the Persian Gulf is planned to be completed in 2002 (*NEFTE Compass*, 10 February 1994).

Iran's hopes with regard to the geopolitics of oil pipelines are being hampered by the enforcement of a rigid US policy of containment against Iran's expanded involvement in the region. This American stance does not seem to be based on the merit of economic developments in the region; rather, it is voiced in general terms: "any idea of an Iranian involvement in the affairs of Caspian–Central Asia – her own region – is not desirable to the United States" (Race, 1995).

Having sifted through dozens of pipeline prospects for over a year, the AIOC, which is predominantly owned by US companies, decided in September 1995 to choose the Russian pipeline option through either Chechnya or Georgia, following the rejection of the most viable route – through Iran (*The Times*, London, as quoted in *Ettelaat International*, 11 September 1995). This choice was based solely on US political considerations. Nevertheless, Iran's short-cut route for exports of Caspian Sea oil makes Azerbaijan stand by its view that it is still possible for the crude oil produced by the AIOC to be exported partly via the Persian Gulf in an Iranian–Azeri oil-swap deal (*Ettelaat International*, 17 March 1995). A similar suggestion was made by Kazakhstan for part of its Tengiz oil field production to be exported through the Persian Gulf in a swap deal with Iran (*Ettelaat International*, 11 October 1995).

In addition, Iran not only started oil exploration in its own Caspian offshore areas in 1995, but also created two exploration companies with Russia and Azerbaijan (*Ettelaat International*, 28 September 1995). The NIOC also signed an agreement with Azerbaijan, whereby the two states agreed to drill for oil in Iran's offshore area (*Ettelaat International*, 7 August 1995).

Of the Caspian and Central Asian republics, Uzbekistan was the only state that subscribed to the US declaration of economic sanctions against Iran. Although some Uzbek officials contradicted others by denying reports that the republic endorsed US sanctions against Iran, the Uzbek republic continued to contravene Iranian policies in Central Asia.

Central Asia

Iran's third northern geopolitical region of concern includes the five newly independent states of Turkmenistan, Kazakhstan, Uzbekistan, Tajikistan, and Kyrgyzstan. This region is connected to the Caspian Sea region because two of the Central Asian nations, Turkmenistan and Kazakhstan, along with Iran itself, border the Caspian Sea.

The Republic of Azerbaijan is the only Muslim state of the Caucasus, which separates it culturally from the other states. Yet this factor, together with Azerbaijan's economic and strategic homogeneity with the Caspian Sea and Central Asian states, links Azerbaijan to the nations of both regions. Inclusion of the Republic of Azerbaijan in the Economic Cooperation Organization (ECO) alongside the Central Asian republics confirms a geopolitical perspective that places Azerbaijan within the broader Caspian–Central Asia region.

ECO membership comprises Azerbaijan, Kazakhstan, Turkmenistan, Uzbekistan, Tajikistan, Kyrgyzstan, and Afghanistan, as well as Iran, Turkey, and Pakistan; the latter three countries are the original members of the ECO's predecessor, the Regional Cooperation Organization (RCD). The ECO was formed in February 1992, and has held annual summit meetings. The leaders of the Islamic Republic of Iran have openly expressed the hope that the ECO would become a regional economic grouping worthy of global competition in the twenty-first century (Rafsanjani, 1995). However, the success of this regional formation is open to doubt, not just because six of the Caspian–Central Asian republics are also members of the CIS, but also because there is not yet the necessary cohesion amongst member states for the level of economic integration required for a serious regional organization. Furthermore, Turkey, an important member of the ECO, does not appear to harbour as much dedication to making this regional organization successful as it does to joining the European Union. Similarly, the bulk of Pakistan's geopolitical attention has centred on the Indian subcontinent, which prevents it from committing fully to the ECO as an economically and politically integrated regional organization. These are the same factors that caused the RCD to fail, after functioning for three decades as an effective regional organization. Thus, Iran has no alternative but to pursue its own geopolitical perspective of a regional organization in Central Asia. A number of factors make the Caspian–Central Asia area worthy of the geographical term "region."

HISTORICALLY. The peoples of Iran, Afghanistan, Tajikistan, Turkmenistan, Uzbekistan, and parts of Kazakhstan, together with most peoples of the Caucasus, have long experience of living together in the commonwealth of the pre-Islamic Achaemenian, Parthian, and Sassanid empires, in the Abbasid caliphate, in the Persian and Turkic empires of the Samanids, Seljhuqids, and Ghaznavids, and, more recently, in the Safavid empire.

CULTURALLY. The experience of more than 2,000 years of interaction among the nations of the Caspian–Central Asia region within a politically united commonwealth has created a cultural conglomeration that binds these nations together in their geographic region. The expansion of Islam eastward added a new impetus to this cultural conglomeration, further strengthening it.

Iran shares a common language with Tajikistan and the majority of the people of Afghanistan and Uzbekistan, and Azerbaijan is now the only other Shiite country in the world besides Iran. Central Asian cities such as Bokhara, Samarkand, Balkh, Merv, Khiva, and Khorezm feature prominently in Persian literature as traditional centres of Iranian arts and science. Finally, millions of fellow Turkmen and Azeris – unscathed by the Russian colonial drive of the nineteenth century – live in the Azerbaijan and Turkmensahra provinces of Iran.

GEOGRAPHICALLY. It is worth observing that all the Muslim republics of the former Soviet Union are landlocked, with little prospect of easy access to the world's oceans. This problem will become more pronounced as the economic independence of those republics gradually becomes full-blown and if the CIS with Slavic and Muslim states fails to be effective. Kazakhstan, Turkmenistan, and Azerbaijan, along with Iran and Russia, have access to the Caspian Sea, which could encourage maritime trade among these states. Such a development would not, however, solve the problem of lack of access (via the sea) to the markets of the world. A practical solution to this geographical fact would be the linking of these republics and Afghanistan to the Persian Gulf and the Gulf of Oman by road, railway, and networks of oil and gas pipelines. With its 2,000 miles of coastline on the Persian Gulf, the Strait of Hormuz, and the Gulf of Oman, Iran is the *only* Central Asian country with free access to the open seas. This could be of great benefit to the landlocked countries of the region as well. Moreover, Iran's vast natural resources, matched by no other neighbouring country, provide a situation that encourages economic and technological cooperation among the states of the region.

In early December 1991 an agreement was signed between Iran and Kazakhstan allowing all Central Asian republics to extend their railway networks to the Persian Gulf via Iran (*Echo of Iran*, December 1991, p. 6). Another agreement signed in the same year with the former Soviet Union, and upheld by the new republics, lifted border obstacles between Azerbaijan and Turkmenistan with Iran. This agreement enabled cross-border peoples of the same ethnic background to travel freely within 45 miles on each side of their borders.

Tripartite cooperation between Iran, Turkmenistan, and Armenia increased dramatically in 1995 and an agreement was signed by these states in June 1995 to expand trade by road transport among the three (*Ettelaat International*, 6 June 1995).

In the presence of the leaders of all Central Asian republics in March 1995 (*Ettelaat International*, 17 March 1995), inauguration of the internal Iranian railway network to the Iranian port of Bandar Abbas on the Persian Gulf – to be linked to the Central Asian railway networks in early 1996 – was a testimonial to Iran's efforts to assume the role described by Kazakh leaders as "the main bridge between Central Asia and the outside world via the Persian Gulf" (*Ettelaat International*, 20 June 1995). To enhance this role, Iran is also seeking to attract India to participate in the expansion of its railway networks. Currently Indian ships use Georgian, Russian, and Ukranian ports in the Crimean Peninsula, and hundreds of kilometres of road through Russia in order to reach Central Asia. Iran has reportedly approached India to fund a 700 km rail stretch between Bafq and Mashhad (*Ettelaat International*, 28 March 1995). Once this stretch is completed, the Persian Gulf–Central Asian connection will have been shortened by several hundred kilometres. This would give India a lead over its neighbours in Central Asia and would tremendously benefit the expansion of its economic (especially trade) links with Central Asia.

ECONOMICALLY. In spite of the progress being made in increasing road and railway links with Central Asia, Iran does not seem to have made much progress in mobilizing the region toward the formation of a regional economic grouping, other than the ECO. In fact, until the end of 1994, it seemed that Iran had lost the battle with Russia for the hearts and minds of the former Soviet republics. This loss resulted from the combined effect of political and economic shortcomings, which prevented Iran from making the kind of commitment that these republics needed to enhance their political and economic independence. Added to this is a determined US–Israeli policy of blocking the expansion of Iranian influence in the region (*Ettelaat International*, 1 November 1995). Competition from Russia and rivalries with Turkey, Pakistan, and Saudi Arabia have made it difficult for Iran to achieve its northern geopolitical aspirations.

To overcome a situation of near-impasse, Iran on the one hand seems to have formulated new strategies based on views closer to those of Russia and, on the other, has expanded bilateral and trilateral relations with the Central Asian republics.

The emergence in 1995 of a coordinated Russo-Iranian political front in the Caspian–Central Asia region facilitated the expansive roles of both countries there. Apart from the repeated Russian confirmation of continued nuclear and technological cooperation with Iran (to the displeasure of the United States), the two countries agreed in October 1995 to set up a joint company for oil projects in which other countries could also participate (*Ettelaat International*, 1 November 1995).

Together, Iran, Russia, and Central Asia have 54 per cent of the world's natural gas deposits. Exploitation of these resources and their export through an elaborate pipeline network would, from the Iranian point of view, enhance its northern geopolitical strategy and, therefore, its key position in the emerging global political hierarchy.

An agreement signed in September 1994 between Iran and Turkmenistan will realize the construction of a gas pipeline from Central Asia to Europe via Iran to be completed in 25 years; Iran will cover 50 per cent of the costs. This line is scheduled to be completed in two phases, initially carrying an annual 10–12 billion m^3 of gas, which will then be increased to 28–30 billion m^3 in the second phase (*Daily Ettelaat*, 22 Septemter 1994). Another agreement signed in Tehran in July 1995 provides for a second line connecting Turkmenistan to existing Iranian gas lines. A 200 km pipeline will be constructed, 60 km of which will be on Iranian territory (*Ettelaat International*, 7 July 1995). Iran also signed an agreement with India in August 1995, whereby India will be connected to the Iranian and Central Asian gas fields through a 2,000 km pipeline (*Ettelaat International*, 4 August 1995). This network will undoubtedly play a major future role in linking the Caspian–Central Asia region to gas and oil consumers on the Indian subcontinent and in the Far East.

Pakistan has been pressing hard for a share in this future by trying to become connected to Iranian and Central Asian gas fields. Having secured understandings with Iran in this regard, Pakistan reached agreement with Turkmenistan in October 1995 whereby a gas pipeline would connect Pakistan to Central Asia via Afghanistan (*Ettelaat International*, 12 October 1995). This will prove to be a major link in the emerging multinational gas pipeline networks originating from Iran and Central Asia. However, Afghanistan's lack of security will prove to be a major obstacle to the implementation of a trans-Afghanistan pipeline project.

On the political front, sharing political views about the Caspian–Central Asia region with Russia enabled Iran to bring about a preliminary cease-fire agreement in Tehran, on 19 July 1995, between the pro-Russia government leaders of Tajikistan and leaders of Tajikistan's Islamic opposition. In a separate development, Tajik leaders have urged for defence cooperation with Iran (*Ettelaat International*, 2 November 1995). Furthermore, Iran signed a Memorandum of Understanding with Turkmenistan and Tajikistan whereby economic, political, and cultural cooperation among the three would start within a new framework (*Ettelaat International*, 13 September 1995). It is hoped that this will serve as the foundation upon which viable Iran–Central Asian regional integration will develop. The three states have emphasized that their regional cooperation could serve as a suitable model for sustainable economic development and could restore peace and stability in the region (*Ettelaat International*, 13 September 1995, quoting the leaders at the tripartite meeting in Ashkhabad).

These shared historical, cultural, geographical, and economic factors are aspects of a relatively homogeneous environment that could constitute a geopolitical region. A common market in this region, with the geographical and economic advantages of each country complementing the others, is an ideal prospect that could take the whole region as an economic group into the twenty-first century.

The issue of Lake Hamun and the Hirmand River

In the eastern part of Iran, on the southern edge of Central Asia, a major environmental disaster has been in progress during the past 90 years. Lake Hamun (Hamun is an ancient Persian word meaning "lake") was apparently a much larger lake in the past than it is now. It has gradually diminished and with it almost the whole of a water-related local economy has gone. Not only is Lake Hamun the only source of irrigation water in Sistan Province other than the Hirmand River, but it has played a pivotal role for the population in this corner of Central Asia. With an area of 8,117 km^2 of very fertile soil and a population of over 274,000 (Census Taking Centre of Iran, 1986, p. 1), the district of Sistan is virtually dependent on Lake Hamun and its only perennial tributary, the Hirmand River (Hirmand is also an ancient Persian term meaning "abundant in water"). The Hirmand is the tenth-largest river in Asia and drains much of Afghanistan. The main delta branch of the Hirman forms international boundaries between Iran and Afghanistan. Having been described with great exaggeration at the turn of the twentieth century as a lake of 150,000 sq. miles (Tate, 1909, p. 237), Lake Hamun has been reduced to four small pools of water today, with a total surface area of less than 1,200 km^2. This slow-onset, low-grade, but cumulative environmental disaster is the result of a series of policies implemented in Afghanistan regarding the use of Hirmand River water.

The problem began in 1872, when British General Goldsmid delimited the boundary line between Iran and Afghanistan along the main branch of the river. This situation was further aggravated in 1905 when British Colonel McMahon's water resource arbitration awarded two-thirds of the Hirmand delta water to Afghanistan and one-third to the more heavily cultivated, more densely populated Sistan in Iran. As friendly relations developed in the 1930s between the newly independent government of Afghanistan and the centralized government of Iran, the two countries signed an agreement (1939) that divided Hirmand delta water equally between the two (Iran–Afghanistan Treaty of Hirmand Water Division, 1939, Articles I and II). This agreement, however, was ignored by Afghanistan, and the dispute deepened as a number of American companies were given concessions in 1945 by the Afghans for the construction of diversion dams and canals, which further reduced the amount of water reaching the Iranian province of Sistan and Lake Hamun.

The Hirmand River's average annual flow in the 1990s has been estimated at 2–3 billion m^3 or 70–100 m^3 per second. This figure was further reduced to a mere 45 m^3 per second in 1994, of which only 15 m^3 per second entered Sistan (Omur-e Ab-e Sistan, 1995, p. 6).

Although the regionally influential Iranian government of the 1970s settled many territorial differences with its neighbours to the satisfaction of Iranian claims (i.e. Iran regained control of the three islands of Tunbs and Abu Musa in the Persian Gulf in 1971 and established a river boundary with Iraq on the thalweg of Shatt al-Arab in 1975), its very poor showing in this period in its border disputes with Afghanistan remains a mystery. In 1973, Iran signed an agreement with Afghanistan whereby Iran would receive 22 m^3 per second of Hirmand water as its share, and would purchase an additional 4 m^3 per second, bringing its total to 26 m^3 per second,[1] which was substantially less than the one-third amount awarded to Iran in 1905 by McMahon's arbitration. This unusual water treaty failed to become official, owing to the Afghan *coup d'état* of that year. It was justified by Iranian officials of the Pahlavi regime on the ground that "more important" Iranian geopolitical considerations pertained to relations with Afghanistan. The justification was that Iran not only gave Afghanistan what it wanted with respect to Hirmand River water, but also provided US$300 million in financial aid, and road and railway concessions for Afghanistan's access to the Persian Gulf. Iran also promised further financial and economic assistance in order to encourage Afghanistan to withdraw from Soviet influence and join the Western camp as a satellite of Iran.[2]

The disastrous collapse of the Soviet occupation of Afghanistan resulted in a protracted civil war that continues today. The involvement of the Islamic Republic of Iran in Afghan politics is no longer motivated by hydropolitical considerations regarding the Hirmand River and Lake Hamun, but is to foster the emergence of a friendly Islamic regime in that country.

The creeping environmental catastrophe taking place on the southern edge of Central Asia is almost an exact repeat of the Aral Sea catastrophe. Flooding in the Hirmand delta and the restoration of Lake Hamun in recent years do not represent a change of policy; they are the consequence of diminished politico-administrative and technical controls in Afghanistan. These improvements are likely to be only temporary until the completion of the construction of the Kamal Khan diversion dam, which will likely deepen the environmental catastrophe in Sistan and will exacerbate the rift between Iran and Afghanistan.

Conclusion

In light of the changing global geopolitical structure following the demise of communism, Iran has assumed an extremely important role as the landmass that bridges two very important oil regions of the world – the Caspian Sea and the Persian Gulf.

In its diplomatic overtures to the republics of the Caucasus, the Caspian region, and Central Asia, the Islamic Republic of Iran has been trying hard to emphasize economic rather than ideological and political motives. Genuinely concerned about the breakdown of security on its northern border, it has so far brokered at least two cease-fires in the conflict between Azerbaijan and Armenia over Nagorno-Karabakh, and two cease-fires in the Tajikistan civil war.

Depending on (1) the socio-political flexibility of the existing political structure of Iran, (2) its conceptual capacity to give top priority to the geographical aspects of its national interests over ideological considerations in its foreign and regional policies, and (3) its ability to create a well-organized administrative system that would improve its image, Iran will be able to emerge as a significant regional political power as well as an economic success story. Moreover, Iran could decide to make major changes in its foreign and domestic policies. If so, Iran could become a major regional power with the ability to create a successful regional grouping. The formation of any regional grouping, however, will depend on Iran's skill in settling geographical differences with neighbours and its ability to strengthen ties to them. No doubt, an improved image for Iran would be the most effective instrument for changing the political attitude of

121

the United States toward Iranian national interests in the Caspian–Central Asia and Persian Gulf regions.

Notes

1. Private notes sent to me by Mahmud Forughi, Iran's Ambassador in Afghanistan in the late 1960s and early 1970s, who negotiated the 1973 agreement.
2. Statements made to me on Saturday, 4 April 1992, by Dr. Alinaghi Alikhani, a former Minister of Economy and a high-level official of the government of Imperial Iran between 1965 and 1971.

References

Barimani, A. 1947. *Dariay-e Khazar* [The Caspian Sea]. Tehran: Entesharat-e Rangin.

Census Taking Centre of Iran. 1986. *General Census of 1986*, vol. 142–3, Tehran.

Ghorban, N. 1994. "Middle East Petroleum and Gas Conference in Bahrain (16–18 January 1994)." *Iranian Journal of International Affairs* VI (1 and 2).

Iran–Afghanistan Treaty of Hirmand Water Division. 1939. Author's private collection (in Persian).

Khodadov, A. 1995. Statements by the representative of the Russian Foreign Ministry to the seminar on the Caspian Sea held in London, 24 February.

Mojtahed-Zadeh, P. 1992. *The Changing World Order and the Geopolitical Regions of the Persian Gulf and Caspian–Central Asia*. London: Urosevic Foundation Publications.

Omur-e Ab-e Sistan. 1995. A report by the Governorate of Zabul, February/March. Courtesy of Mr. Mohtadi of the Centre for Middle East Scientific Research and Strategic Studies, Tehran.

Race, G. 1995. Statement by the representative of the US State Department to the seminar on the Caspian Sea held in London, 24 February.

Rafsanjani, A. A. 1995. "Address by President Rafsanjani of the Islamic Republic of Iran to the third summit meeting of ECO, Islamabad." *Ettelaat International*, 15 March 1995.

Soviet Business Intelligence Bureau. 1993. *Monthly Journal*, East Consult/Moscow, special report on Central Asia, June.

Tate, G. P. 1909. *The Frontier of Baloochistan – Travel on the Border of Persia and Afghanistan*. London: Witherby.

Part IV
The Dead Sea

10

Principles for confidence-building measures in the Jordan River watershed

Aaron T. Wolf

Introduction

Since regional water talks began in May 1992 in Vienna, Austria, in the context of multilateral negotiations between Arabs and Israelis, the inhabitants of both banks of the Jordan River have been meeting on and off to see if, after years of unilateral development, they can treat the watershed as nature designed it – one integral unit. It has long been known by hydrologists and demographers, and is increasingly recognized by policy makers, that a political solution cannot be reached among Israel, its Arab neighbours, and Palestinians of the West Bank and Gaza without addressing regional water shortages. However, because watershed planning lends itself to a regional approach, and because issues of water are also tied to issues of regional security and immigration, resolving conflict over water may become the most tractable of the subjects to be dealt with during regional peace negotiations. Resolving water conflicts could provide the opportunity for the confidence-building steps necessary to reach accord over other, more contentious, topics as well.

This chapter summarizes the hydropolitical conflict between the riparians of the Jordan River watershed, evaluates methods for achieving equity in water rights claims, and provides some options for water projects to be developed in cooperation-inducing stages, as changing political developments allow.

I first survey the current hydropolitical positions of the co-riparians as well as the physical hydrography of the region. I then describe the current status of international water law and the legal challenges of Jordan River hydropolitics. Borrowing from "dispute systems design," a comparatively recent sub-field of alternative dispute resolution (ADR), I go on to describe how water projects may be implemented in cooperation-inducing stages – the principles for confidence-building. The challenge for political leaders in the watershed is putting these principles into practice. The final section describes many of the technical and policy options that have been proposed both to increase water supply and to decrease water demand in the region. These technical and policy options are organized to be developed step-wise, with greater benefits accruing with greater regional cooperation.

Background

The fluctuating waters of the ancient Middle East have given rise to legend, extensive water law, and the roots of modern hydrology: the flood experienced by Noah is thought to have centred its devastation around the Babylonian city of Ur, submerging the southern part of the Euphrates for about 150 days, while the code of King Hammurabi contains as many as 300 sections dealing with irrigation. The practice of field surveying was invented to help harness the flooding Nile (El-Yussif, 1983). In addition, the waters of the region were occasionally intertwined with military strategy as, for instance, when Joshua directed his priests to stem the Jordan's flow with the power of the Ark of the Covenant, while he and his army marched across the dry river bed to attack Jericho (Joshua 4).

In the centuries since, the inhabitants of the region and the conquering nations that flourished and disappeared have lived mostly within the limits of their water resources, using combinations of surface and well water for survival and livelihood (Beaumont, 1991, p. 1). At the beginning of the twentieth century, as the competing nationalisms of Jews and Arabs began to re-emerge from the ruins of the Ottoman empire, the quest for resources took on a new and vital dimension.

In the years that followed World War I, the location of water resources influenced the boundaries, first between the British and French mandate powers that acquired control over the region, and then between the states that developed subsequently. The Zionist border formulation for a "national home" presented at the Paris Peace Talks in 1919, for example, was determined by three criteria: historic, strategic, and economic, with economic considerations being defined almost entirely by water resources. The entire Zionist programme of immigration and settlement required water for large-scale irrigation and, in a land with no fossil fuels, for hydropower. The development plans, and the boundaries that were required, were "completely dependent" on the acquisition of the "headwaters of the Jordan, the Litani River, the snows of Hermon, the Yarmuk and its tributaries, and the Jabbok" (Ra'anan, 1955, p. 87).

Between World Wars I and II, water became the focus of the greater political argument over how to develop the budding states around the Jordan watershed, particularly Israel and Jordan, and what the "economic absorptive capacity" would be for immigration. Development plans included the Ionides Plan (1939), a British study that suggested that water would be a limiting factor for any additional immigration to Palestine, and the Lowdermilk Plan (1944), which suggested in contrast that, with proper water management, resources would be generated for 4 million refugees in addition to the 1.8 million Arabs and Jews living in Palestine at the time. British policy makers came down on the side of the Ionides Plan, invoking "economic absorptive capacity" to limit Jewish immigration and land transfers for the duration of World War II.

As the borders of the new states were defined, sometimes by warfare, in the 1950s and 1960s, each country began to develop its own water resources unilaterally. On the Jordan River, the legacy of the Mandate and the 1948 Arab–Israeli war was a river divided in a manner in which conflict over water resource development was inevitable. By the early 1950s, Arab states were discussing organized exploitation of two northern sources of the Jordan – the Hasbani and the Banias (Stevens, 1965, p. 38). The Israelis also made public their All Israel Plan, which included the draining of Huleh Lake and swamps, diversion of the northern Jordan River, and construction of a carrier to the coastal plain and Negev Desert – the first out-of-basin transfer for the watershed (Naff and Matson, 1984, p. 35).

In 1951, Jordan announced a plan to irrigate the East Ghor of the Jordan Valley by tapping the Yarmuk. At Jordan's announcement, Israel closed the gates of an existing dam south of the Sea of Galilee and began draining the Huleh swamps, which lay within the demilitarized zone with Syria. These actions led to a series of border skirmishes between Israel and Syria, which escalated during the summer of 1951 (Stevens, 1965, p. 39). In July 1953, Israel began construction on the intake of its National Water Carrier at the Daughters of Jacob Bridge (Gesher B'not Ya'akov) north of the Sea of Galilee and in the demilitarized zone. Syria deployed its armed forces along the border and artillery units opened fire on the construction and engineering sites (Cooley, 1984, pp. 3 and 10). Syria also protested to the United Nations and, although a 1954 resolution for the resumption of work by Israel carried a majority, the USSR vetoed the resolution. The Israelis then moved the intake to its current site at Eshed Kinrot on the north-western shore of the Sea of Galilee (Garbell, 1965, p. 30).

Against this tense background, President Dwight Eisenhower sent his special envoy Eric Johnston to the Middle East in October 1953 to try to mediate a comprehensive settlement of the Jordan River system allocations (Main, 1953). Johnston's initial proposals were based on a study carried out by Charles Main and the Tennessee Valley Authority (TVA) at the request of the United Nations to develop the area's water resources and to provide for refugee resettlement.

The major features of the Main Plan included small dams on the Hasbani, Dan, and Banias, a medium-size (175 million m^3 storage) dam at Maqarin, additional storage in the Sea of Galilee, and gravity-flow canals down both sides of the Jordan Valley. The Main Plan did not include the Litani River and described only in-basin use of the Jordan River water, although it conceded that "it is recognized that each of these countries may have different ideas about the specific areas within their boundaries to which these waters might be directed" (Main, 1953). Preliminary allocations gave Israel 394 million m^3 (MCM) per year, Jordan 774 MCM/yr, and Syria 45 MCM/yr.

Both Israel and a united Arab League Technical Committee responded with their own counterproposals, and Johnston worked until the end of 1955 to reconcile these proposals in a Unified Plan amenable to each of the states involved. In the Unified Plan, Johnston accomplished no small degree of compromise. Although they had not met face to face for these negotiations, all states agreed on the need for a regional approach. Israel gave up on inclusion of the Litani and the Arabs agreed to allow an out-of-basin transfer. The Arabs objected, but finally agreed, to storage at both the Maqarin Dam and the Sea of Galilee, so long as neither side would have physical control over the share available to the other. Israel objected, but finally agreed, to international supervision of withdrawals and construction. Allocations under the Unified Plan, later known as the Johnston Plan, included 400 MCM/yr to Israel, 720 MCM/yr to Jordan, 132 MCM/yr to Syria, and 35 MCM/yr to Lebanon (US Department of State, unpublished summaries, 1955, 1956; see also Naff and Matson, 1984, p. 42).

The technical committees from both sides accepted the Unified Plan, but forward momentum died out in the political realm; the plan was never ratified. Nevertheless, Israel and Jordan have generally adhered to the Johnston allocations, and technical representatives from both countries continue to meet two or three times a year at "Picnic Table Talks" (named for the site at the confluence of the Yarmuk and Jordan Rivers where the meetings are held) to discuss flow rates and allocations (Wolf, 1995).

As each state developed its water resources unilaterally their plans began to overlap. By 1964, for instance, Israel had completed enough of the construction of its National Water Carrier that actual diversions from the Jordan River basin to the coastal plain and the Negev were imminent. Although Jordan was also about to begin extracting Yarmuk water for its East Ghor Canal, it was the Israeli diversion that prompted President Nasser to call for the First Arab Summit in January 1964 of the heads of state from the region and North Africa, specifically to discuss a joint strategy on water.

The options presented at the Summit were to complain to the United Nations, to divert the upper Jordan tributaries into Arab states (as had been discussed by Syria and Jordan since 1953), or to go to war (Schmida, 1983, p. 19). The decision to divert the rivers prevailed at a Second Summit in September 1964, when the Arab states agreed to finance a Headwater Diversion project in Lebanon and Syria and to help Jordan build a dam on the Yarmuk. They also made tentative military plans to defend the diversion project (Shemesh, 1988, p. 38).

In 1964 Israel began withdrawing 320 MCM/yr of Jordan water for its National Water Carrier and Jordan completed a major phase of its East Ghor Canal (Inbar and Maos, 1984, p. 21). In 1965, the Arab states began construction of their Headwater Diversion Plan to prevent the Jordan headwaters from reaching Israel. The plan was to divert the Hasbani into the Litani in Lebanon and to divert the Banias into the Yarmuk, where it would be impounded by a dam at Mukhaiba for Jordan and Syria. This plan would divert up to 125 MCM/yr, cut by 35 per cent the installed capacity of the Israeli Carrier, and increase the salinity in the Sea of Galilee by 60 parts per million (ppm) (US Central Intelligence Agency, 1962; Inbar and

Maos, 1984, p. 22; Naff and Matson, 1984, p. 43). The Israeli army attacked the diversion works in Syria in March, May, and August of 1965.

These events set off what has been called "a prolonged chain reaction of border violence that linked directly to the events that led to the [June 1967] war" (Safran cited in Cooley, 1984, p. 16). Border incidents continued between Israel and Syria, triggering air battles in July 1966 and April 1967 and, finally, all-out war in June 1967.

With the territorial gains and improvements in geostrategic positioning that Israel achieved in the June 1967 war, Israel also improved its "hydrostrategic" position (see fig. 10.1). With control of the Golan Heights, it now held all of the headwaters of the Jordan, with the exception of a section of the Hasbani, and an overlook over much of the Yarmuk. Together these made the Headwaters Diversion impossible. The West Bank now controlled by Israel not only provided riparian access to the entire length of the Jordan River but it overlay three major aquifers, two of which flow west and north-west into Israel and had been tapped into from Israel's side of the Green Line since 1955 (Garbell, 1965, p. 30). The third flows east to the Jordan Valley. Jordan had planned to transport 70–150 MCM/yr from the Yarmuk River to the West Bank; these plans were abandoned.

When Israel took control of the West Bank and Gaza in 1967, the territory it captured included the recharge areas for the three aquifers. The entire renewable recharge of the first two aquifers is already being exploited and the recharge of the third is close to being depleted as well. In the years of Israeli occupation, a growing West Bank and Gaza population, along with burgeoning Jewish settlements, have increased the pressures on the limited groundwater supply, resulting in an exacerbation of already tense political relations. Palestinians have objected strenuously to Israeli control of local water resources and to the development of settlements that they see as being at their territorial and hydrological expense (see, for example, Davis et al., 1980; Dillman, 1989; Zarour and Isaac, 1993). Israeli authorities view hydrological control in the West Bank as defensive. With about 30 per cent of Israeli water originating on the West Bank, the Israelis perceive the necessity to limit groundwater exploitation in these territories in order to protect the resources themselves and their wells from salt-water intrusion (Gruen, 1991).

By 1991, several events combined to shift the emphasis on the potential for "hydro-conflict" in the Middle East to the potential for "hydro-cooperation." The first event was a natural one, but limited to

Fig. 10.1 **The Jordan River: International borders, 1967 to the present, and water diversions (Source: Wolf, 1995)**

the Jordan basin. Three years of below-average precipitation caused a dramatic tightening in the water management practices of each of the riparians, including rationing, cut-backs to agriculture by as much as 30 per cent, and the restructuring of water pricing and allocation. Although these steps placed short-term hardships on those affected, they also showed that, for years of normal rainfall, there was still some flexibility in the system. Most water decision makers agree that these steps, particularly regarding pricing practices and allocations to agriculture, were long overdue.

The next series of events were geopolitical and region-wide. The Persian Gulf War in 1990 and the collapse of the Soviet Union caused a realignment of political alliances in the Middle East that finally made possible the first public face-to-face peace talks between Arabs and Israelis, in Madrid, Spain, on 30 October 1991. During the bilateral negotiations between Israel and each of its neighbours, it was agreed that a second track should be established for multilateral negotiations on five subjects deemed "regional," including water resources. Although the pace of the peace talks has been at times arduously slow,[1] a venue does finally exist where grievances can be aired and the issue of water-sharing equity can be tackled. In itself, this may help prevent some of the pressures that have historically led to some of the most bitter water conflicts in the world.

Hydrography

Surface water

The Jordan River watershed drains an area of 18,300 km^2 in four countries: Lebanon, Syria, Israel, and Jordan (Naff and Matson, 1984, p. 21).

Three springs make up the northern headwaters of the Jordan River: the Hasbani, rising in Lebanon with an average annual flow of 125 MCM/yr, the Banias in Syria, averaging 125 MCM/yr, and the Dan, the largest spring at 250 MCM/yr and originating in Israel. The streams from these springs converge 6 km into Israel and flow south to the Sea of Galilee at 210 m below sea level.[2]

The Yarmuk River has sources in both Syria and Jordan and forms the border between those countries before it adds about 500 MCM/yr to the Jordan 10 km south of the Sea of Galilee. Beyond this confluence, the Jordan picks up volume from springflow and intermittent tributaries along its 320 km meander southward along the valley floor of the Syrio-African Rift. At its terminus at the Dead Sea (400 m below sea level), the Jordan River has a natural annual flow of 1,400 MCM/yr.

Because much of the Jordan's flow is below sealevel and the small springs that contribute to its flow pass first through the salty remains of ancient seas, the salinity of the water rises greatly, even as its flow increases. Although the headwaters at the Hasbani, Banias, and Dan have a salinity of 15–20 ppm, the level at the south end of the Sea of Galilee is 340 ppm. This is diluted somewhat by the Yarmuk, which has a salinity of 100 ppm, but increases significantly downstream, reaching several thousand parts per million by the Allenby Bridge near Jericho. The Dead Sea, a terminal lake, has a salinity of 250,000 ppm, seven times that of the open ocean.

The Jordan River flows through the transition zone from the Mediterranean subtropical climate of Lebanon and the Galilee region in the north to the arid conditions of the Negev Desert and the Rift Valley to the south. Rainfall patterns likewise vary spatially, with rainfall decreasing generally from north to south and from west to east.

These streamflow values are for *average* flows of the natural system. The actual amounts are highly variable and dependent on both seasonal fluctuations (75 per cent of precipitation falls during the four winter months) as well as inter-annual variations in rainfall (as high as 25–40 per cent) (Environmental Protection Service, 1988, p. 125). Also, the natural system has been dramatically altered by large-scale diversion projects, discussed later.

Groundwater

The hills along both banks of the Jordan serve as recharge areas for extensive aquifer systems in the West Bank, Israel, and Jordan. Rain that falls on these mountain ridges and that does not run off as surface water percolates down to the water table, contributing to these underground bodies of water. One measure of an aquifer's utility is its *safe yield*, or the amount of water that can be pumped without adverse effects on the water left in storage. This is usually considered to be equal to the annual recharge rate for the aquifer.

There are three principal aquifer systems west of the Jordan (Kahan, 1987, p. 21); see figure 10.2. The north-east basin recharges in the northern West Bank and discharges in Israel's Bet Shean and Jezreel Valleys; it has a safe yield of 140 MCM/yr. The western

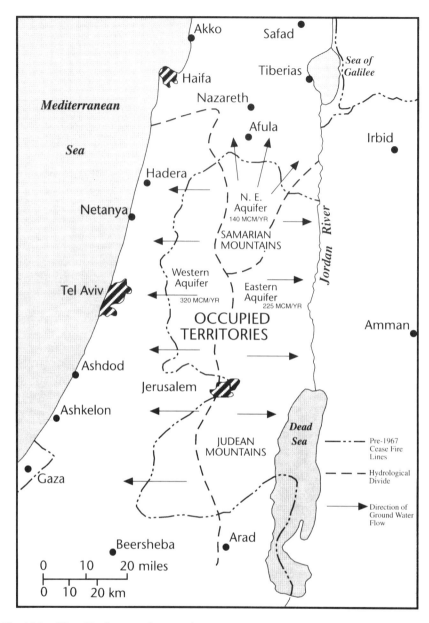

Fig. 10.2 **West Bank groundwater: Average annual sustainable yields for the three principal aquifers west of the Jordan River (Source: Wolf, 1995)**

134

(Yarkon–Tanninim) basin also recharges in the hills of the West Bank but discharges westward, toward the Mediterranean coast in Israel; it has a safe yield of 320 MCM/yr. The eastern basin is made up of five separate catchment areas in the West Bank, all of which flow east toward the Jordan Valley; their combined safe yield is 225 MCM/yr.[3]

Groundwater replenishment within Jordan totals about 270 MCM/yr, in 12 different aquifers, mostly in the Zarqa, Yarmuk, and Jordan catchments (Bilbeisi, 1992).

Current water use

Israel has a renewable annual water supply of approximately 1,800 MCM/yr (Environmental Protection Service, 1988, p. 125), of which 60 per cent is groundwater and 40 per cent is surface water – almost entirely from the Jordan River system. Its annual water budget is allocated 73 per cent to agriculture, 22 per cent to domestic consumption, and 5 per cent to industrial use. Israel irrigates 66 per cent of its cropland. It has a population of 4.2 million and an annual population growth rate of 1.6 per cent (excluding immigration) (Postel, 1989a, p. 12).

The 800,000 Palestinians on the West Bank consume about 110 MCM/yr, 90 per cent of which is groundwater. Of this, about 90 MCM is for irrigation and the rest is for domestic use. The 70,000 Israeli settlers use an additional 36 MCM, 95 per cent of which is for agriculture (Kahan, 1987, p. 113). The Arab and Jewish residents of the West Bank irrigate 6 per cent of the cultivable land and have a population growth rate of approximately 3 per cent (Postel, 1989a, p. 14).

Gaza, with a population of about 600,000 and a growth rate of 3.4 per cent, is probably the entity that is most desperate hydrographically speaking. Completely dependent on the 60 MCM/yr of annual groundwater recharge, Gazans currently use approximately 95 MCM/yr. The difference between annual supply and use is made up by overpumping in the shallow coastal aquifer, resulting in dangerous salt-water intrusion of existing wells and ever-decreasing per capita water availability, already the lowest in the region.

Jordan has a total annual water budget of 870 MCM, of which 75 per cent is surface water, mostly from the Yarmuk River (Taubenblatt, 1988, p. 49). Of the total, 85 per cent is allocated for agriculture, 10 per cent for human consumption, and 5 per cent for industrial use. Jordan irrigates 10 per cent of its cropland and has a population of 3.3 million and a growth rate of 3.5 per cent per year (Postel, 1989a, p. 14).

Both Lebanon and Syria are relatively minor consumers of Jordan River water. Their major sources are the Litani and Euphrates rivers, respectively. The Litani, with an average flow of 700 MCM/yr, lies wholly within Lebanon but, because it flows to within 7 km of the Hasbani, it has been included in several diversion schemes in conjunction with the Jordan system. Lebanon irrigates 29 per cent of its cropland and has a population of 2.6 million and an annual population growth rate of 2.1 per cent. Syria irrigates 11 per cent of its cropland and has a population of 10 million growing at a rate of 3.8 per cent per year (Postel, 1989a, p. 14).

International water rights law

General principles

One problem at the heart of Middle East water conflicts is the fact that there is no internationally accepted definition of water-sharing equity. International water law is ambiguous and often contradictory, and no mechanism exists to enforce principles that are agreed upon.

According to Cano (1989), international water law did not begin to formulate substantially until after World War I. Since that time, organs of international law have tried to provide a framework for increasingly intensive water use. The concept of a "drainage basin," for example, was accepted by the International Law Association in the Helsinki Rules of 1966, which also provides guidelines for "reasonable and equitable" sharing of a common waterway (Caponera, 1985). Article IV of the Helsinki Rules describes the overriding principle.

Each basin State is entitled, within its territory, to a reasonable and equitable share in the beneficial uses of the waters of an international drainage basin.

Article V lists no fewer than 11 factors that must be taken into account in defining what is "reasonable and equitable."[4] There is no hierarchy to these components of "reasonable use." Rather, they are to be considered as a whole. One important shift in legal thinking in the Helsinki Rules is that they address the right to "beneficial use" of water, rather than to water *per se* (Housen-Couriel, 1992, p. 5).

The International Law Commission, a body of the United Nations, was directed by the General Assembly in 1970 to study "Codification of the Law on Water Courses for Purposes Other Than Navigation." It is testimony to the difficulty of marrying legal and hydrologic intricacies that the International Law Commission, despite an additional call for codification at the UN Water Conference at Mar de Plata, Argentina, in 1977, has not yet completed its task. After 20 years and 9 reports, only several articles have been provisionally approved. And, once the details are worked through, the principles would not have the force of law until approved by the UN General Assembly (Solanes, 1987). Even then, cases are heard by the International Court of Justice only with the consent of the parties involved; no practical enforcement mechanism exists to back up the Court's findings, except in the most extreme cases. A state with pressing national interests can, therefore, disclaim entirely the Court's jurisdiction or findings (Caponera, 1985; Cano, 1989).

Treaties and river commissions

In contrast to the development and application of a general law code, treaties and river commissions have been established and perpetuated for water systems throughout the world. According to Rogers (1991) there are more than 200 river basins shared by two or more countries. This accounts for more than 50 per cent of the land area of the earth. More than 280 treaties have been negotiated to resolve these trans-boundary water conflicts. Treaties are brought about either directly between the parties involved, i.e. by negotiation, or with the help of a third party, i.e. by mediation. Once ratified, a treaty has the force of law and is the highest precedent recognized by the International Court of Justice (Cano, 1989).

Treaties and river commissions have reached a certain level of success, probably because they fill precisely the gaps left in generalized international water law. They address only local conditions and incorporate the vested interests of the specific parties in conflict. The initial process still requires a certain amount of good will on both sides or, barring that, particularly strong encouragement from a third party. The challenge is to get the parties together initially and, once there, to induce ongoing cooperation. This is a process best served by alternative dispute resolution strategies, as addressed in the following sections. But, as professor of law Robert Hayton concludes, "just as war is too important to be left to the generals, water law is too important to be left to the lawyers" (1982, p. 132).

The legal challenges of Jordan River hydropolitics

Shifting riparian positions
Given the difficulty of defining the rights of riparians in international law, one can imagine the compounded complications of applying such a code where the riparian positions, and resulting legal claims, continue to shift over time. Lebanon, Syria, and Jordan were all upper riparians between 1948 and 1967, and their corresponding legal claim, therefore, was mostly of "absolute sovereignty" of the Jordan River. This conflicted, during the Johnston negotiations (1953–1955), with the US desire for "optimum development" and with the Israeli claim to its "riparian rights." Because Jordan was somewhat restrained, being also a lower riparian further downstream, a compromise Arab claim was of rights to water allocation proportional to a territory's contribution to its source (Lowi, 1985).

From 1964 to 1967, Syria and Lebanon began building a diversion of the Jordan headwaters, again claiming "absolute sovereignty," to thwart a downstream Israeli diversion that threatened the Jordanian water supply. Jordan challenged the Israeli plan to move water out-of-basin, arguing that it was entitled to the river's "absolute integrity" and that first priority should be given to in-basin uses (Naff and Matson, 1984). After 1967, Israel became the upper, and predominant, riparian and moved towards a claim of "absolute sovereignty," although remaining, for the most part, within the confines of the (unratified) Johnston allocations.

Complicating riparian positions even further has been the unresolved issue of groundwater. Israel currently receives about 30 per cent of its water budget from aquifers that recharge in the West Bank. Ownership and rights to this water are in conflict, with Israel claiming "prior appropriation," limiting Palestinian groundwater development in the West Bank. Palestinians have objected to this increasing control. Legal arguments often refer, at least in part, to the Fourth Geneva Convention's discussion of territories under military occupation (see, for example, Dillman, 1989; El-Hindi, 1990). In principle, it is argued, the resources of occupied territory cannot be exported to the benefit of the occupying power. Israeli authorities reject these arguments, usually claiming that the Convention is not applicable to the West

Bank or Gaza because the powers these territories were wrested from were not, themselves, legitimate rulers. Egypt was itself a military occupier of Gaza and only Britain and Pakistan recognized Jordan's 1950 annexation of the West Bank. Also, it is pointed out that the water Israel uses is not being exported but rather flows naturally seaward, and, because Israel has been pumping that water since 1955, it has "prior appropriation" rights to the water. Both Israel and Jordan insist that any further allocation to the West Bank must come out of the other's share.

Recognition of state sovereignty

As mentioned previously, an international legal code is applicable only to states that adhere to a court's jurisdiction. This principle, however, runs into two types of problems in the Jordan watershed:

1. *States.* Arab state recognition of Israel's right to exist has come only recently. One reason given for the collapse of the Johnston negotiations was that ratification would have implied recognition of Israel's legitimacy (Wishart, 1990). Israel, in turn, has not, until recently, recognized the national aspiration of Palestinians, who, in the absence of sovereign territory, have been relegated to observer status in most international forums.
2. *Jurisdiction.* As mentioned above, Palestinians have claimed that much of Israeli action on the West Bank, including control of water resources, violates the Geneva Convention protecting civilians under military occupation (Ataov, 1981). Israel rejects the applicability of the Convention to these territories, claiming that, since Jordanian annexation of the West Bank in 1950 was not widely recognized in the international community, the Israeli presence is, thus, not legally "occupation."

Thus, submission of the dispute over the Jordan River to the international legal system would strain existing interpretation and enforcement well past their current limits.

Cooperative watershed development

Principles for confidence-building

Given the vital need for a regional water development plan that incorporates the political realities of the region and given the limitations imposed by economics and hydrologic conditions, steps that might be taken are described below.

A recently developed sub-field of alternative dispute resolution (ADR) called "dispute systems design" focuses on a process for integrating the potential for ADR into public institutions and other organizations that deal with conflict. Dispute systems design as described by Ury et al. (1988) may offer lessons about enhancing cooperation in water systems as well. Although most of the work in this field describes the incorporation of cooperation-inducement into organizations, some of the same lessons for "enhancing cooperation capacity" (Kolb and Silbey, 1990, p. 300) or "design considerations" (O'Connor, 1992, p. 87) and "design guidelines" (McKinney, 1992, p. 160) might be applicable to technical or policy-making systems as well. For example, a water-sharing agreement, or even a regional water development project, might also be designed from the beginning specifically to induce ever-increasing cooperation as the project incorporates ever-increasing integration.

The preceding survey of history suggests that cooperation-inducing strategies might also be incorporated into the process of implementation. This section offers examples of "cooperation-inducing implementation." General guidelines include the following:

1. *"Dis-integrating" the control of water resources to address past and present grievances.* Many plans for water development in the Jordan River watershed incorporate the premise that the increased integration of institutions or water projects is an impetus to greater political stability.[5] Although the advisability of striving towards ever-increasing integration is recognized, as is the fact that "lasting peace among nations is characterized by a broadly based network of relations" (Ben-Shahar, 1989, p. 1), it is nevertheless suggested that, for resource conflicts in general and for water conflicts in particular, it should first be ensured that each entity has adequate control of an equitable portion of its primary resource. Thus, past and present grievances need to be addressed, before embarking on projects of cooperation or integration.

   Because much of the past conflict over water has concerned ambiguous water rights, any attempt at developing cooperative projects that precedes the clarification of these rights would be building on years of accumulated ill will. The clear establishment of property rights is also a prerequisite for any market solutions that might be applied, such as water banks or markets. Furthermore, as mentioned previously, the political viability of international planning or projects depends on each entity agreeing on the equity of the project (e.g. who gets how much) and on control of the resource (who exercises control, and from where). Necessary steps include:

- negotiating property rights to existing resources,
- guaranteeing control of a water source adequate to meet future needs, and
- addressing the issue of equity within the design of any cooperative project.

Since these steps involve a separation of control over resources as a precondition to "integration," this process might be referred to as "dis-integration."

2. *Examining the details of initial positions for options to induce cooperation*. Each of the parties to negotiations usually has its own interests foremost in mind. The initial claims, or "starting points" in the language of alternative dispute resolution, often seek to maximize those interests. By closely examining the assumptions and beliefs behind the starting points, one might be able to glean clues about how to induce some movement within the "bargaining mix," or range within which bargaining can take place, for each party. These underlying assumptions (and beliefs) may also provide indications for the creative solutions necessary to move from distributive (e.g. "win–lose") bargaining over the amount of water each entity should receive to integrative (e.g. "win–win") bargaining, i.e. inventing options for mutual gain.

3. *Designing a plan or project, starting with small-scale implicit co-operation and building towards ever-increasing integration, always "leading" political relations*. Building on the first two steps, riparians of a watershed who have clear water rights and control of enough water for their immediate needs might begin to work slowly toward increasing their cooperation on projects or planning. It has been shown that even hostile riparians can cooperate if the scale is small and the cooperation is secret. Building on that small-scale cooperation, and keeping the concerns about equity and control firmly in mind, projects might be developed to increase integration within the watershed, and over time even between watersheds.

In addition to these three principles, a viable agreement should also incorporate mechanisms to cope with future misunderstandings that will need to be resolved. The circumstances that bring about a conflict are seldom static; neither are the conditions that bring about agreement. This is particularly true for hydrological conflicts, where supply, demand, and understanding of existing conditions change from season to season and from year to year. Finally, crisis management for droughts, floods, and technical failures (e.g. dam or sewage facility) must also be addressed.

The design of a plan or project can incorporate a feedback loop to allow for greater cooperation as political relations develop, encouraging the project to remain always on the cutting edge of political relations. A process for ongoing conflict resolution would also help to relieve tensions that might arise because of fluctuations in the natural system. This process of "cooperation-inducing-design" can be applied to water rights negotiations, to watershed planning, or to the development of cooperative projects for watershed development.

Technological and management alternatives for the future

There is an entire array of solutions to water resource limits, ranging from agricultural to technological to economic and public policy, but they all fall under the same two basic categories as for any resource shortage: increase supply or decrease demand. Allowance must also be made for anticipated climatic and demographic shifts.

Increasing supply

New natural sources
No new "rivers" will be discovered in the Middle East, but increased catchment of winter floodwater anywhere along the existing river system can add to the region's water budget. This applies to small wadis as well as to large storage projects such as the Maqarin Dam, which alone could contribute savings of about 330 MCM/yr. When it is possible to store water underground through artificial groundwater recharge (e.g. not lost to evaporation), even more water is saved. Less evaporation also reduces the salinity in the remaining water. Israel currently stores 200 MCM/yr from its National Water Carrier project through this method (Ambroggi, 1977).

Underground is the only place to look for any real new water supplies. In 1985, Israel confirmed the discovery of a large fossil aquifer in the Nubian sandstone underlying the Sinai and Negev deserts. It is already exploiting 25 MCM/yr from this source and is investigating the possibility of pumping up to 300 MCM/yr in the twenty-first century (Issar, 1985). Jordan has also been carrying out a systematic groundwater evaluation project in recent years, with the help of the

United States Agency for International Development and the US Geological Survey (Starr and Stoll, 1988, p. 32).

Any other regional source of water would have to come at the expense of another watershed. Despite this, at one time or another Israel has eyed the Litani and the Nile, Jordan has looked to the Euphrates, and all of the countries in the area have been intrigued by the "Peace Pipeline," proposed by Turkey in 1987. The western line of this project would deliver 1,200 MCM/yr from the Seyhan and Ceyhan rivers to Syria, Jordan, and Saudi Arabia (Duna, 1988, p. 119). Despite Turkish Prime Minister Ozal's belief that, "by pooling regional resources, the political tensions in the area can be diffused" (Duna, 1988, p. 121, quoting Prime Minister Ozal), the idea did not gain rapid popularity because of its cost of US$20 billion.

New sources through technology
Projects such as iceberg towing and cloud seeding, though appealing to the imagination, do not seem to be the most likely direction for future technology. The former involves great expense and the latter can at best be a small part of a very local solution. Although a representative of Israel's water authority claims that 15 per cent of Israeli annual rainfall is due to its cloud-seeding programme (Siegal, 1989, p. 12), this has been documented only within the northern Galilee catchment and results seem not to have the consistency necessary for reliable water resources planning.

The two most likely future technologies to increase water supply are desalination and wastewater reclamation. The Middle East has already spent more on desalination plants than any other part of the world. The region has 35 per cent of the world's plants, with 65 per cent of the total desalting capacity, mostly along the Arabian peninsula (Anderson, 1988, p. 4). Israel, too, included plans for both conventional and nuclear desalination plants in its water planning until 1978, when they were abandoned as "technologically premature and economically unfeasible" (Galnoor, 1978, p. 352).

Desalinated water is expensive for most applications. Although drinking water is a completely inelastic good – that is, people will pay almost any price for it – water for agriculture, by far the largest use in the Middle East, has to be cost-effective enough so that agricultural end-products remain competitive in the market-place. The present costs of about US$0.80–1.50/m^3 to desalt sea water and about US$0.30/m^3 for brackish water (Awerbuch, 1988, p. 59) do not make this technology an economic water source for most uses. Efforts are being made, however, to lower these costs through multiple-use plants (getting desalted water as a by-product in a plant designed primarily for energy generation), increased energy efficiency in plant design, and augmenting conventional plant power with solar or other energy sources.[6]

One additional use of salt water is to mix it with fresh water in just the right amount so as to leave it useful for agricultural or industrial purposes, in effect freeing up water to be added to the freshwater supply. This method was used in Israel in the 1975/76 season to add 141 MCM/yr to the water budget (Kahhaleh, 1981).

Another promising technology to increase supply is wastewater reclamation. Two plants in Israel currently treat 110 MCM/yr or 40 per cent of the country's sewage for re-use, and projections call for treating 80 per cent by the end of the 1990s (Environmental Protection Service, 1988, p. 8). The treated water is currently used to irrigate some 15,000 hectares, mostly cotton (Postel, 1989b, p. 42). It is anticipated that full exploitation of purified waste water will eventually constitute 45 per cent of domestic water needs (Environmental Protection Service, 1988, p. 147). This type of project could be developed throughout the region (a World Bank loan helped finance the Israeli project). An obvious limitation of this technology is directly related to the amount of waste water generated by a population in a year.

Decreasing demand

The guiding principle to decrease demand for any scarce resource should be, "Can it be used more efficiently?" This does not always work, however, especially when there is an emotional value associated either with the resource or with the proposed solution. Unfortunately, when dealing with water, emotions usually charge both aspects of the issue. For example, the most direct way to cut demand for Middle East water is to limit population growth in the region. However, in an area where each national group and religious and ethnic subgroup seems to be locked in some demographic race for numerical superiority, this is not likely to occur. Many of the sectors most susceptible to efficient restructuring are also those most laden with emotion.

The agricultural sector
Some aspects of decreasing agricultural water demand are non-controversial and have made the region a showcase for arid-agriculture

water conservation. Technological advances such as drip-irrigation and micro-sprinklers, which reduce water loss by evaporation, are about 20–50 per cent more efficient than standard sprinklers and tremendously more so than the open-ditch flood method used in the region for centuries (Environmental Protection Service, 1988, p. 144). Computerized control systems, working in conjunction with direct soil moisture measurements, can add even more precision to crop irrigation.

Other water savings have come through bio-engineered crops that exist on a minimal amount of fresh water, on brackish water, or even on the direct application of salt water.[7]

Economic water efficiency
Water distribution in the Middle East is so riddled with economic inefficiencies that an economist approaching it must feel very much like a drip-irrigation designer watching a field being flood-irrigated. The main problem is that the cost of water to the user is highly subsidized, especially with regard to water that has been earmarked for agriculture. The true cost of water would reflect all of the pumping, treatment, and delivery costs of that water, most of which are not passed on to the farmers. In Israel alone, 20 per cent of the country's energy is used solely to move water from one place to another (Naff and Matson, 1984, p. 12).

Economic theory argues that only when the price paid for a commodity is a reasonable reflection of the true price can market forces work for efficient distribution of the commodity.[8] In other words, subsidized water leads to waste in agricultural practices, too little incentive for research and development of conservation techniques and practice, and, finally, too much water being allocated to the agricultural sector as opposed to industry. Take away subsidies and allow the price to rise, it is argued, and market incentives are created for both greater efficiency on the farm and a natural shift of water resources from the agricultural sector to industry, where contribution to GNP per unit of water is often much higher (Wishart, 1989, p. 49). Since in each of the areas discussed between 75 per cent and 95 per cent of water use is allocated for agricultural use, savings could be substantial.

Economic analysis may also create a framework for easing regional water tensions. "Put simply, conflicts over water rights are easier to resolve if transaction costs of resolution are lower, and if opportunities exist for improving the efficiency of water use and discovery"

(Wishart, 1989, p. 50). In other words, if it is cheaper for people to cooperate and save water than it is to fight, they would rather cooperate.

There are, however, problems inherent in using economic theory as the tool for water conflict analysis, problems that can lead to weaknesses in the economic solutions prescribed. First, water is not a pure economic good. Options to the consumer of most goods include migrating to where it is cheaper if so desired or abstaining from it altogether if the price is too high. Given small countries with tightly controlled borders, the former is not a viable alternative, nor, for more obvious biological reasons, is the latter. Presumably, though, the analysis is restricted to water for agriculture, where there is ample room for reducing demand before running into such dangers.

The second problem is more serious because it has to do with a force much more fundamental than economic theory, that is, the emotions of a nation. All of the countries in the area were built from the farm up, and the agriculturalist, whether the *fellah* or the *kibbutznik*, holds a special mystique on both sides of the Jordan. Both Arabic and Hebrew ideologies are rife with slogans of "making the desert bloom" and "nations rooted in their land." In this context, water invariably becomes the "lifeblood" of a nation. One result of this has been a certain political and financial leeway granted to agriculture in the area.

Even while recognizing its limits, one can still use economic analysis as a useful tool to provide some guidelines to increase hydrological efficiency. And it has been suggested that following these guidelines can be especially crucial as water limits begin to be reached.

Public policy
Where the "invisible hand" of economic forces fails to guide a more efficient water use, authoritative guidelines of public policy can take over. Government agencies could, after all, simply implement one analyst's prescription of cutting water to agriculture by 35 per cent if they wished (Naff, 1990). The "if they wished" is the problem. The same national water ethics that give agriculture great economic clout in the region, also give it great political clout. The Water Commission in Israel, for example, is the ultimate authority for all water planning and operations in the country. It, in turn, is controlled by the Ministry of Agriculture. Clearly there is room for improvement even in terms

of national public policy. But the real opportunities come from the international policy sector.

Water policy in this region is currently drawn up within the boundaries of a nation rather than within those of a watershed. Because the flow of water does not respect political boundaries, it should be clear that regional management, at least at the watershed level, would be a much more efficient approach. In fact, the only point on which the water policy analyses surveyed here do agree is on the need for planned water sharing and joint water development, as Eric Johnston had envisioned 35 years ago.

Regional cooperation would open the door to a host of new water distribution alternatives.[9] For example, surface water from the Yarmuk or the upper Jordan could be provided to the West Bank, allowing increased development in that area, while alleviating Israeli fears of overdrafted Palestinian wells. Or Israel and Jordan might cooperatively develop both banks of the Jordan, eliminating the current redundant costs of separate delivery systems within each country. And, the larger the region cooperating, the more efficient can be a regional plan. It is cheaper, for example, to bring water from the Nile to the Negev than it is to pump it from the Kinneret, as is the current practice (Kally, 1989, p. 305).

Despite Kally's contention that "the successful implementation of cooperative projects ... will strengthen and stabilize peace" (1989, p. 325), this does not necessarily seem to be the case. It seems at this point inconclusive whether greater interdependence is actually an impetus to greater cooperation or is, in fact, the opposite, leading to greater conflict. Many of the hostilities that have occurred in the region over water seem to have come about precisely because the water destined to a downstream user was controlled by an upstream party. Many "cooperative" projects might only provide additional opportunity for suspicion and potential for contention. Lowi (1993) suggests that issues of regional water sharing cannot be successfully broached until the larger political issues of territory and refugees are resolved.

However, the fact that projects would have to be weighed in terms of the conflict-alleviating tendencies of more efficient water distribution, as opposed to the possible conflict heightening of greater hydrological interdependence, should not be a reason to abandon the concept. Nor should the concept of a regional planning approach be tarnished because of uncertainty about specific projects.

Climatic and demographic shifts

An analysis of such a fragile "hydropolitical" situation as exists in the Middle East is actually more complicated than so far discussed. This is because so few of the parameters that are examined remain stable for any length of time. Aside from the volatile nature of politics in general, and Middle East politics specifically, two other factors complicate the present precarious situation, one climatic and one demographic.

Many climatologists are currently investigating the kinds of changes that might occur in regional climatic and weather patterns, given the projected increase of a few degrees Celsius in the average global temperature. One climate scenario suggests a possible north-ward shift in the distribution of winter rainfall away from the Jordan basin. Difficult though they are to predict on a regional scale, the effects of shifting annual precipitation patterns in the Middle East could have profound impacts on the politics of the region, depending on how dramatic the changes are that actually develop. As global and regional modelling and forecasting efforts improve, appropriate planning measures will have to be taken.

A second, more imminent, change is already beginning to occur in the region, which will dramatically affect water distribution and usage. Israel expects at least 1 million Soviet immigrants in the coming decade, possibly 2 million. Jordan is absorbing 300,000 Palestinians who left Kuwait in the aftermath of the Gulf War. Furthermore, if political negotiations were to result in an autonomous Palestine on the West Bank, that entity might absorb a percentage of the 2.2 million Palestinians now registered worldwide as refugees (Jaffee Center for Strategic Studies, 1989, p. 206). Based on current consumption, Israel would require an additional 94 MCM/yr (or a little over 5 per cent of its current water budget) just to provide for personal use by 1 million immigrants. Jordan would need an additional supply of 17.5 MCM/yr for its refugees, and the West Bank would need an additional 25 MCM/yr (a 23 per cent increase in its water budget) to provide for the personal water needs of 1 million immigrants.[10]

These numbers represent simple extrapolations based on current water use. However, given the fact that hydrological limits in the region are currently being reached and that annual supplies are routinely being surpassed, questions about the absorptive capacity of the region's water resources for immigrants and refugees must be raised.

Recommendations

The inextricable link between water and politics suggests several options for easing regional tensions related to water issues.

First, efficient water use should be enhanced as much as is politically, economically, and technologically possible. Increased efficiency should strive for the following:

- *Regional water resource planning on the watershed scale.* In the case of the Jordan River, representatives from Lebanon, Syria, Jordan, Israel, and the West Bank should be working together on watershed management planning. For greater efficiency, the geographical scale of planning could be increased. Planning options multiply as the planning scale and the sources of water resources increase. Allowances should be made for changes in climate and demographics.
- *Increased economic efficiency through a shift of water used from agricultural to industrial sectors.* Although some observers have recommended a shift of as much as 35–40 per cent (Naff, 1990), the states involved have security concerns that may preclude their becoming major food importers, even if it were more economical to do so. These concerns will likely be weighed when determining how much of a shift is warranted.
- *Increased support for research and development of water-saving technology.* This should include such small-scale applications as low-flow shower nozzles and toilets, and such large-scale projects as sequential re-use and wastewater treatment for the agricultural and industrial sectors. The Maqarin Dam should be built. Special emphasis might be placed on small- and large-scale desalination technology. A regional desalination project, based on the goals of the agro-industrial complex and using a combination of solar, natural gas, and hydropower (rather than nuclear), might be implemented to achieve many of the regional benefits that were foreseen in the original plan.[11]

Secondly, issues of water scarcity must be included in regional political negotiations in order for any resulting agreements to have long-term viability. This is particularly true of the Israeli–Palestinian conflict, where any separation of the two entities generates intricate problems of hydrological viability for both parties.

Third parties such as the United States, Russia, and the European Union have vital roles to play in these strategies: information barriers can be more easily broken down on neutral territory; funding for cooperative projects will most likely have to be raised outside of the region; and opportunities for dialogue will have to be provided and encouraged to facilitate the pace of peace negotiations.

Conclusions

The Jordan River watershed, with all its competing national and economic pressures, provides a clear example of the strategic importance of water as a scarce resource. If emphasis is placed on easing regional water tensions, some breathing space might be gained, allowing for more complex political and historical difficulties to be negotiated. Because the water problems to be solved involve all of the parties in conflict, and because these issues are so fundamental, the search for regional solutions might actually be used as a tool to facilitate cooperation. People who cannot talk together about history or politics might talk about water if their lives and economies depended on it.

The present "hydropolitical" situation in the Middle East is one of intricate problems and delicate solutions. The equitable distribution of scarce water resources in the Jordan River watershed is particularly precarious. Both the dangers of conflict and the opportunities for cooperation are growing, as annual supplies are being surpassed.

Acknowledgements

I would like to thank the United Nations University for its sponsorship of the Central Eurasian Water Forum, and Professors Kobori and Glantz for their careful editing of this volume. This work is drawn from Wolf (1995).

Notes

1. For an update on the Middle East peace talks as related to water resources, see Bingham et al. (1994).
2. Flow data are taken from Bakour and Kolars (1994), Garbell (1965), Inbar and Maos (1984), Naff and Matson (1984), p. 182.
3. Not included in this list are the Carmel aquifer, lying wholly in Israel, with a safe yield of 375 MCM/yr, or the sandstone Gaza aquifer, whose 80 MCM/yr yield is currently being seriously overmined.
4. The factors comprise a basin's geography, hydrology, climate, past and existing water utilization, economic and social needs of the riparians, population, comparative costs of alternative sources, availability of other sources, avoidance of waste, practicability of compensation as a means of adjusting conflicts, and the degree to which a state's needs may be satisfied without causing substantial injury to a co-basin state.
5. See, for example, proposals by Kally (1989). Kally contends that "the successful implementation of cooperative projects ... will strengthen and stabilize peace" (p. 325). This

concept of inducing increasing integration even between actors with some hostility toward each other is also a strategy employed in the United States by the US Army Corps of Engineers, recommended for international settings by Corps representatives.

6. For good information on non-conventional desalination projects, see Murakami (1995).
7. For interesting examples of direct sea-water irrigation, see Hodges et al. (1988).
8. Wishart (1989) provides a good economic analysis of Jordan River water.
9. Most of the following projects are described in detail in Kally (1989).
10. All of the numbers provided here are direct extrapolations of the data provided in the section of this paper entitled "Current water use."
11. For the past decade, the Israelis have sought to build a canal from the Mediterranean Sea that would provide 800 MW of hydro-power by dropping 800 MCM/yr of salt water 400 m at the Dead Sea, the lowest point on earth. Such a Med–Dead Canal would also make possible power generation in "solar ponds," a new technology that takes advantage of heat trapped in the lower layer, which has much higher salinity than that of the Mediterranean. If the focus of the canal project became desalination, rather than strictly power generation, and if Negev and Sinai land were to be set aside for reclamation, many of the regional benefits for immigrant/refugee absorption and for political cooperation of the agro-industrial complex could be realized.

References

Ambroggi, R. 1977. "Underground reservoirs to control the water cycle." *Scientific American* 236(5), pp. 21–27.

Anderson, E. 1988. "Water: The next strategic resource." In: J. Starr and D. Stoll (eds.), *The Politics of Scarcity: Water in the Middle East*. Boulder, Colo.: Westview Press.

Ataov, T. 1981. "The use of Palestinian waters and international law." Paper presented at the Third United Nations Seminar on the Question of Palestine, Colombo, Sri Lanka, 10–14 August.

Awerbuch, L. 1988. "Desalination technology: An overview." In: J. Starr and D. Stoll (eds.), *The Politics of Scarcity: Water in the Middle East*. Boulder, Colo.: Westview Press.

Bakour, Y. and J. Kolars. 1994. "The Arab Mashrek: Hydrological history, problems, and perspectives." In: P. Rogers and P. Lydon (eds.), *Water in the Arab World*. Cambridge, Mass.: Harvard University Press.

Beaumont, P. 1991. "Transboundary water disputes in the Middle East." Paper presented at a conference on "Transboundary Waters in the Middle East," Ankara, Turkey, September, mimeo.

Ben-Shahar, H. 1989. "Economic cooperation in the Middle East: From dream to reality." In: G. Fishelson (ed.), *Economic Cooperation in the Middle East*. Boulder, Colo.: Westview Press.

Bilbeisi, M. 1992. "Jordan's water resources and the expected domestic demand by the years 2000 and 2010, detailed according to area." In: A. Garber and E. Salameh, *Jordan's Water Resources and Their Future Potential*. Amman: Friedrich Ebert Stiftung, pp. 7–31.

Bingham, G., A. Wolf, and T. Wohlgenant. 1994. *Resolving Water Disputes: Conflict and Cooperation in the U.S., the Near East, and Asia*. Washington, D.C.: US Agency for International Development, November.

Cano, G. 1989. "The development of the law in international water resources and the work of the International Law Commission." *Water International* 14, pp. 167–171.

Caponera, D. A. 1985. "Patterns of cooperation in international water law: Principles and institutions." *Natural Resources Journal* 25(3), pp. 563–588.

Cooley, J. 1984. "The war over water." *Foreign Policy* 54, Spring, pp. 3–26.

Davis, U., A. Maks, and J. Richardson. 1980. "Israel's water policies." *Journal of Palestine Studies* 9(2), pp. 3–32.

Dillman, J. 1989. "Water rights in the Occupied Territories." *Journal of Palestine Studies* 19(1), pp. 46–71.

Duna, C. 1988. "Turkey's Peace Pipeline." In: J. Starr and D. Stoll (eds.), *The Politics of Scarcity: Water in the Middle East*. Boulder, Colo.: Westview Press.

El-Hindi, J. L. 1990. "Note. The West Bank aquifer and conventions regarding laws of belligerent occupations." *Michigan Journal of International Law* 11(4), pp. 1400–1423.

El-Yussif, F. 1983. "Condensed history of water resources developments in Mesopotamia." *Water International* 8, pp. 19–22.

Environmental Protection Service. 1988. *The Environment in Israel*. Jerusalem, Israel.

Galnoor, I. 1978. "Water policymaking in Israel." *Policy Analysis* 4, pp. 339–367.

Garbell, M. 1965. "The Jordan Valley Plan." *Scientific American* 212(3), pp. 23–31.

Gruen, G. 1991. *The Water Crisis: The Next Middle East Crisis?* Los Angeles: Wiesenthal Center.

Hayton, R. 1982. "The groundwater legal regime as instrument of policy objectives and management requirements." *Natural Resources Journal* 22(1), pp. 119–139.

Hodges, C. et al. 1988. "Direct seawater irrigation as a major food production technology for the Middle East." In: J. Starr and D. Stoll (eds.), *The Politics of Scarcity: Water in the Middle East*. Boulder, Colo.: Westview Press, pp. 109–118.

Housen-Couriel, D. 1992. "Aspects of the law of international water resources." Draft.

Inbar, M. and J. Maos. 1984. "Water resources planning and development in the northern Jordan Valley." *Water International* 9, pp. 18–25.

Issar, A. 1985. "Fossil water under the Sinai-Negev peninsula." *Scientific American* 253(1), pp. 104–111.

Jaffee Center for Strategic Studies. 1989. *The West Bank and Gaza: Israel's Options for Peace*. Tel Aviv: Tel Aviv University.

Kahan, D. 1987. *Agriculture and Water Resources in the West Bank and Gaza (1967–1987)*. Jerusalem: Jerusalem Post Publishing.

Kahhaleh, S. 1981. *The Water Problem in Israel and Its Repercussions on the Arab–Israeli Conflict*. Beirut: Institute for Palestine Studies.

Kally, E. 1989. "The potential for cooperation in water projects in the Middle East at peace." In: G. Fishelson (ed.), *Economic Cooperation in the Middle East*. Boulder, Colo.: Westview Press.

Kolb, D. and S. Silbey. 1990. "Enhancing the capacity of organizations to deal with disputes." *Negotiation Journal* 6(4).

Lowi, M. 1985. *The Politics of Water: The Jordan River and the Riparian States*. Montreal: McGill Studies in International Development No. 35.

——— 1993. *Water and Power: The Politics of a Scarce Resource in the Jordan River Basin*. Cambridge: Cambridge University Press.

McKinney, M. 1992. "Designing a dispute resolution system for water policy and management." *Negotiation Journal* 8(2).

Main, Charles T. Inc. 1953. *The Unified Development of the Water Resources of the Jordan Valley Region.* Knoxville, Tenn.: Tennessee Valley Authority.

Murakami, M. 1995. *Arid Zone Water Resources Planning for Peace.* Tokyo: United Nations University Press.

Naff, T. 1990. Lecture at University of Wisconsin, Madison, 28 March.

Naff, T. and R. Matson (eds.). 1984. *Water in the Middle East: Conflict or Cooperation?* Boulder, Colo.: Westview Press.

O'Connor, D. 1992. "The design of self-supporting dispute resolution programs." *Negotiation Journal* 8(2).

Postel, S. 1989a. "Trouble on tap." *Worldwatch* 12.

———— 1989b. "Water for agriculture: Facing the limits." *Worldwatch* 39.

Ra'anan, U. 1955. *The Frontiers of a Nation: A Re-examination of the Forces Which Created the Palestine Mandate and Determined Its Territorial Shape.* Westport, Conn.: Hyperion Press.

Rogers, P. 1991. "International river basins: Pervasive unidirectional externalities." Paper presented at a conference on "The Economics of Transnational Commons," University of Sienna, Italy, 25–27 April.

Schmida, L. 1983. *Keys to Control: Israel's Pursuit of Arab Water Resources.* Washington, D.C.: American Educational Trust.

Shemesh, M. 1988. *The Palestinian Entity 1959–1974: Arab Politics and the PLO.* London: Frank Cass.

Siegal, J. 1989. "The world's best rainmaker." *Jerusalem Post*, 8 April.

Solanes, M. 1987. "The International Law Commission and legal principles related to the non-navigational uses of the waters of international rivers." *Natural Resources Forum* 11(4).

Starr, J. and D. Stoll (eds.). 1988. *The Politics of Scarcity: Water in the Middle East.* Boulder, Colo.: Westview Press.

Stevens, G. 1965. *Jordan River Partition.* Stanford, Calif.: Hoover Institution.

Taubenblatt, S. 1988. "Jordan River basin water: A challenge in the 1990's." In: J. Starr and D. Stoll (eds.), *The Politics of Scarcity: Water in the Middle East.* Boulder, Colo.: Westview Press.

Ury, W., J. Brett, and S. Goldberg. 1988. *Getting Disputes Resolved: Designing Systems to Cut the Costs of Conflict.* London: Jossey-Bass.

US Central Intelligence Agency. 1962. "Struggle for Jordan waters." Unpublished memorandum, May.

Wishart, D. 1989. "An economic approach to understanding Jordan Valley water disputes." *Middle East Review* 21(4), pp. 45–53.

———— 1990. "The breakdown of the Johnston negotiations over the Jordan waters." *Middle Eastern Studies* 26(4).

Wolf, A. 1995. *Hydropolitics along the Jordan River: The Impact of Scarce Water Resources on the Arab–Israeli Conflict.* Tokyo: United Nations University Press.

Zarour, H. and J. Isaac. 1993. "Nature's apportionment and the open market: A promising solution convergence to the Arab–Israeli conflict." *Water International* 18(1).

11

Alternative strategies in the inter-state regional development of the Jordan Rift Valley

Masahiro Murakami

Introduction

By the beginning of the twenty-first century, Israel, Jordan, and the West Bank will have depleted virtually all of their renewable sources of fresh water, if current patterns of consumption are not quickly and radically altered. As water shortages occur and full utilization is reached, water policies tend to be framed more and more in zero-sum terms, adding to the probability of discord.

Water conservation and management (including water-pricing scenarios) are essential confidence-building measures to manage the water resources in the region. In these circumstances, non-conventional strategic alternatives, including desalination and the re-use of treated waste water, will become increasingly and significantly important in water resources development to supply new additional fresh water in the twenty-first century.

Energy supplies are closely related to desalination and wastewater treatment for re-use because these treatments consume substantial amounts of electricity. Taking into account recent advances in membrane separation technologies, many countries in the Middle East are also trying to introduce large-scale desalination by the year 2000. Although this is likely to be dependent on low-energy types of

154

reverse osmosis membrane, the energy cost will be 30–50 per cent of the total (Murakami, 1991, 1995). Consequently, the potential use of off-peak electricity will be a key element in minimizing the cost of water management and operation.

The Jordan Valley, which includes the two inter-state regions of the Dead Sea and Aqaba, has become the focus of international cooperation and economic development for peace and confidence building in the aftermath of the "Declaration of Principles" between Israel and the Palestine Liberation Organization (PLO) on 13 September 1993 and the "Treaty of Peace" between Jordan and Israel on 26 October 1994. It is now possible to conceive of an integrated, stepwise regional development plan for the lower Jordan River, the Dead Sea, and Aqaba, including some new, non-conventional alternatives, given the limitations imposed by political frameworks and boundary conditions that exclude the two upstream riparian states of Syria and Lebanon. This chapter assesses three techno-political strategic alternatives to supply fresh and safe drinking water – canal schemes for co-generation, the lower Jordan Peace Drainage Canal, and the Aqaba hybrid sea-water pumped-storage scheme for co-generation – taking into account the incentives for eco-political decision-making, inter-state regional economic development, and the desire for peaceful cooperation.

Canal schemes for co-generation

The best aspects of two types of projects – the regional approach with emphasis on international economic cooperation, and the comparatively safe and clean energy applications of the Med–Dead (Mediterranean–Dead Sea; MDS) Canal or the Red–Dead (Red Sea–Dead Sea) Canal – might be combined, integrated with new co-generation technology, and expanded for a new hybrid project for water and power. The project could also be incorporated into a badly needed regional water development plan for the Middle East, in particular to supply fresh and safe drinking water in the region.

The core of the complex might be either a Med–Dead or a Red–Dead Canal (see fig. 11.1), with a new emphasis on reverse osmosis desalination fuelled by direct hydro-pressure in a topographical head difference. In contrast to earlier plans, which focused on power generation and unilateral development, a new approach would make available, in sparsely populated areas, power and water for fish ponds, industry, and even recreation on artificial lakes, to the benefit

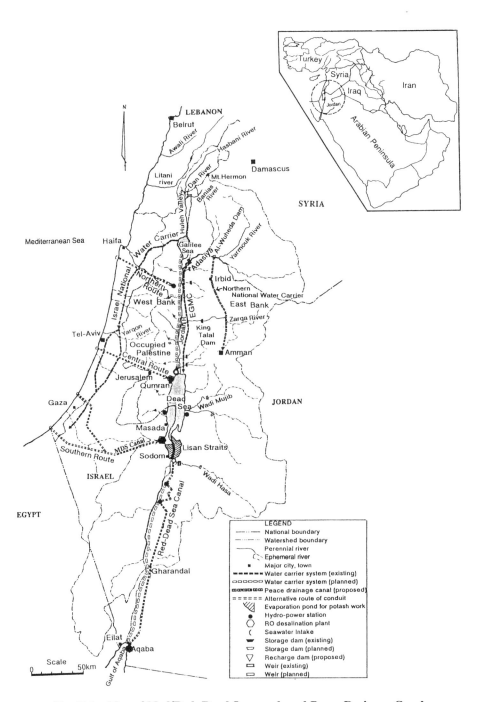

Fig. 11.1   **Map of Med/Red–Dead Sea canals and Peace Drainage Canal**

156

of populations from Egypt, Israel, Jordan, Gaza, and the West Bank. The scope of the project could expand, depending on cost, financing, and which of the countries and territories of the region were to be involved; greater benefits would accrue with larger-scale involvement. Either way, the focus on water, rather than power, and an emphasis on cooperative regional development instead of unilateral benefits, could add both the economic and the political viability that earlier plans lacked.

The original Med–Dead salt-water canal would have been sited in a particularly favourable position to foster regional cooperation. The intake would have been located in or near the Gaza Strip, which is the site of some of the most squalid and densely populated refugee camps in the world, as well as of severe groundwater overdraft. The Canal itself would have run parallel to the Egyptian–Israeli border and then into the Negev and Sinai deserts. A Red–Dead route would provide similar opportunities for Jordanians and Israelis.

The Med–Dead route and the Red–Dead route would each face obvious obstacles in terms of political viability, as have all plans for regional cooperation. The Mediterranean (Gaza)–Dead Sea Canal was revived in the "Declaration of Principles" on 13 September 1993, in which the Annex on the Protocol on Israeli–Palestinian cooperation concerning regional development programmes suggests as a priority the techno-political project of the Med–Dead Canal.

Conceptual design

The 400 m drop at the Dead Sea could be used not only for hydropower generation but also for reverse osmosis desalination. This single pressure of 40–60 kg/cm^2 would be directly used to convert sea water for drinking purposes at a reasonable treatment cost of less than US$1/m^3. The topography and geology of the Red–Dead route do not favour the combination of hydropower generation with a reverse osmosis desalination plant in a single-pressure pipeline system that requires terminal end pressure of 40–60 kg/m^2. The Med–Dead conduit route (Gaza–Masada), on the other hand, is ideal for adding a reverse osmosis desalination plant at the end of the pressure pipeline system on the existing design.

Co-generation refers to the use of waste heat from a conventional (oil or coal) energy-producing plant for the desalination of sea water. The co-generation scheme was first conceived to provide both hydroelectricity and fresh water from reverse osmosis sea-water desalination plants in the early 1980s (Glueckstern, 1982). The use of a part of the hydro potential to make reverse osmosis desalination cost-effective was shelved, however, owing to high costs and a poor understanding of membrane technologies at the time (WPDC, 1980, 1983).

Discussion of the MDS in the early 1980s might not have sufficiently emphasized the idea of shared resources and the benefit of joint development, given political limitations at the time. Indeed, until now, there had been no attempt at comprehensive development of the Jordan River system, which includes the linkage of MDS and the Al-Wuheda dam on the Yarmouk tributary. This new co-generation approach to the MDS scheme thus takes into account both recent innovative developments in membrane technology for reverse osmosis (RO) desalination, which aim to save energy and to make reverse osmosis desalination more cost-effective, and recent changes in the Middle East political situation following the Gulf War in March 1992, the Israel–PLO Declaration of Principles in September 1993, and the Jordan–Israel Treaty of Peace in October 1994, which may make comprehensive basin development not only technically and financially feasible but politically desirable and, indeed, urgent.

Hydro-powered sea-water reverse osmosis desalination for co-generation would exploit the elevation difference of 400 m between the Mediterranean and the Dead Sea (see figs. 11.1 and 11.2). The Dead Sea water level would be maintained at a steady-state level with some seasonal fluctuations of about 2 metres to sustain the sea-water level between 402 m and 390.5 m below mean sealevel, during which inflow into the Dead Sea should balance evaporation.

The bilateral (or trilateral) development plan of the Israel/Palestine (Jordan) Mediterranean–Dead Sea conduit scheme (IJMDS) is a co-generation alternative that would combine a solar–hydro scheme with a hydro-powered sea-water reverse osmosis desalination plant as illustrated in fig. 11.2. The IJMDS scheme would have six major structural components:

– an upstream reservoir (the Mediterranean) at zero sealevel, with essentially an infinite amount of water,
– a sea-water carrier by tunnel, canal, and pipeline, with booster pumping station,
– an upper reservoir and surge shaft at the outlet of the sea-water carrier to allow or regulate the water flow,
– a storage-type hydroelectric unit capable of reverse operation to allow the system to work also as a pumped-storage unit, if required,

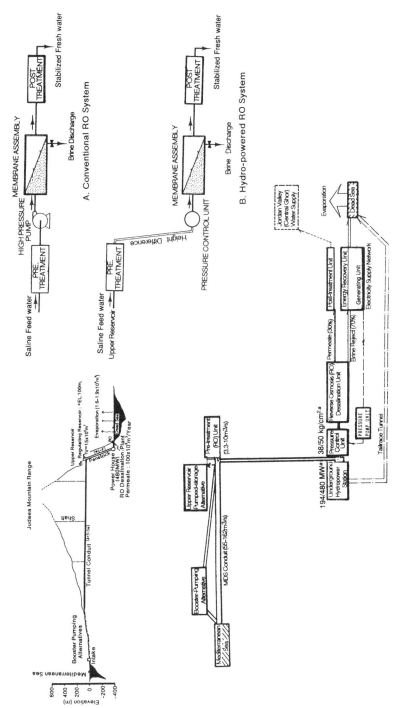

Fig. 11.2 Schematic profile of MDS canal for co-generation (Note: *a.* pumped storage alternative)

159

– a downstream reservoir (the Dead Sea), at a present surface elevation of approximately 400 m below sealevel,
– a hydro-powered reverse osmosis desalination plant, including a
pre-treatment unit, a pressure control unit, the reverse osmosis
unit, an energy recovery unit, a post-treatment unit, and regulating
reservoirs for distribution.

The theoretical hydro potential to exploit the head difference
between the Mediterranean Sea ($=0$ m) and Dead Sea ($=-400$ m)
by diverting $56.7 m^3$/sec. (1.6 billion m^3 per year) of sea water is estimated to be 194 MW. The hydropower plant would produce 1.3 billion kWh per year of electricity with installed capacity of 495 MW
assuming peak-power operation. These figures coincide with the plan
of the Tahal consultancy company in 1981 (Tahal, 1982).

A booster pumping alternative could be applied to make an effective head difference of 500 m, taking into account the operating water
pressure at 50 kg/cm^2 and cheap electricity during off-peak periods.
The sea-water diversion capacity is estimated to be 50 m^3/sec., comprising 39 m^3/sec. of intake water for the hydro-power unit and 11 m^3/
sec. of feed water for the desalination unit.

The hydropower unit has a theoretical hydro potential of 160 MW,
and it generates 1.2 billion kWh per year of electricity with installed
capacity of 480 MW and operating at peak power for 8 hours a day.
To produce 100 million cubic meters (MCM) per year of permeate
(water filtered through a membrane), the installed capacity of the
reverse osmosis plant is estimated to be 322,300 m^3/day (with a load
factor of 85 per cent; Murakami, 1991, 1993).

Marginal operation of the reverse osmosis system is designed to
use the hydro-potential energy in a tunnel conduit (penstock) with
481.5 m of effective head of water for 16 hours a day off-peak (see
fig. 11.3). The feedwater requirements to produce 100 MCM per year
of permeate with 1,000 mg/litre of total dissolved solids (TDS) are
estimated to be 333 MCM per year, assuming a 30 per cent recovery
ratio. The brine reject of 233 MCM a year, whose salinity is 57,000 mg/
litre of TDS, is then discharged into the Dead Sea (Murakami, 1991,
1993). The energy recovery potential from the brine reject is estimated to be 28,280 kW, assuming 20 per cent of friction loss in the
reverse osmosis circuit.

The annual production of electricity from the reverse osmosis brine
reject is estimated to be 168 million kWh with a load factor of 68 per
cent. The recovered energy (electricity) will be used to supply elec-

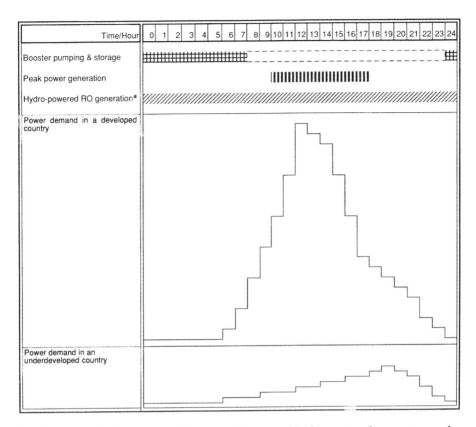

Fig. 11.3 **Marginal operation of pumped-storage and hydro-powered reverse osmosis desalination (Note: *a*. reverse osmosis desalination operating for 16 hours per day)**

tricity for the post-treatment process or other purposes to save electricity on the national grid.

These estimates of hydro potential are based on conventional equations as shown below:

$$Pth = 9.8^*Ws^*Q^*He \tag{1}$$

$$P = Pth^*Ef \tag{2}$$

$$Pp = P^*(24/8) \tag{3}$$

$$Py = 365^*24^*Gf^*P \tag{4}$$

$$Per = 9.8^*Ws^*Qbr^*He^*(1 - Fro)^*Ef, \tag{5}$$

where Pth = theoretical hydro potential (kW)
      Ws = specific weight of feed water ($= 1.03$–1.05)
      Q = flow discharge (m³/sec.)
      He = effective head of water difference (m)
      P = installed capacity (kW)
      Ef = synthesized efficiency ($= 0.85$)
      Pp = installed capacity for 8 hours a day of peak operation (kW)
      Py = potential power generation (output) per year (kWh)
      Gf = generating efficiency ($= 0.85$)
     Per = installed capacity of energy recovery unit (kW)
     Qbr = brine reject water from reverse osmosis membrane module (m³/sec.)
     Fro = hydraulic friction loss in the reverse osmosis circuit ($= 0.2$ or 20%)

Cost estimates

The project costs of the proposed reverse osmosis unit are pre-liminarily estimated to be US$389.4 million capital expenditure and US$44.4 million per year for operation and maintenance. The cost estimates are based on 1990 prices, assuming: a plant life of 20 years, a membrane life (replacement) of 3 years, 8 per cent interest during the three years of construction, the exclusion of cost benefits from energy recovery, and the exclusion of the costs of source water and pipeline/distribution (Murakami, 1991, 1993). The unit water cost of hydro-powered sea-water reverse osmosis desalination to produce 100 MCM/yr is estimated to be US$0.63/m³, which is reasonable when compared with international water tariffs and the estimated unit water cost of US$0.85–1.07/m³ in the "Peace Pipeline" project, and/or the estimated unit water cost of US$1.6/m³ by conventional reverse osmosis desalination using electricity to create pressure of 50–60 kg/cm² (Murakami, 1991, 1993).

The Peace Drainage Canal scheme and eco-political decision-making

The lower Jordan system (including the Dead Sea), which is shared by three riparians – Israel, Palestine (West Bank), and Jordan (East Bank) – will be an area of focus to demonstrate the willingness for peace through economic development. The "Peace Drainage Canal"

(PDC) scheme, which would salvage brackish water, including saline spring water and irrigation return in the Jordan Valley, is proposed not only to protect the water quality of the lower Jordan mainstream but also to produce new fresh potable water (Murakami and Musiake, 1994). The PDC scheme would have an 85 km drainage canal along the lower Jordan River in either the West Bank or the East Bank, and a brackish water reverse osmosis desalination plant with an installed capacity of 200,000 m^3 per day at the terminal end of the canal system (fig. 11.4). The reverse osmosis desalination plant would convert useless or harmful saline waters into safe potable water at reasonable cost, taking into account incentives generated by eco-political decision-making to share the resources and benefits among the three riparians.

Conceptual design

The PDC scheme is being proposed to take into account the following six planning elements with eco-political decision-making initiatives:
1. *Water environment.* Freshwater quality and the ecosystem of the lower Jordan system would be conserved by diverting the harmful saline water that at present is being wasted in the mainstream, adversely affecting downstream users in Palestine (West Bank) and Jordan (East Bank).
2. *Feedwater source.* Brackish waters including saline spring water, base flow, and brackish groundwater in the Jordan Valley would be collected from the three riparian states. Israel would salvage saline spring water in Lake Tiberias and in and around Beit She'an. Palestine and Jordan would collect saline spring water, irrigation returnflow, deep percolation, saline groundwater in the shallow sandy aquifer, and brackish groundwater in the Jordan Rift Valley in the deep sandstone aquifer.
3. *Joint water management.* Diversion intake, infiltration pond, and a dual-purpose well system would be incorporated in a plan to salvage 50–100 MCM of residual winter flows in the lower Jordan system for joint use. The dual-purpose wells would mainly be sunk in the sandy shallow aquifer system. Tubewells that could pump 25–50 MCM per year of brackish groundwater from the deep sandstone aquifer system would be added to supply feed water during the dry season (fig. 11.5).
4. *Drainage canal system and reverse osmosis plant.* An 85 km drainage canal would collect saline water from Israel, the West Bank,

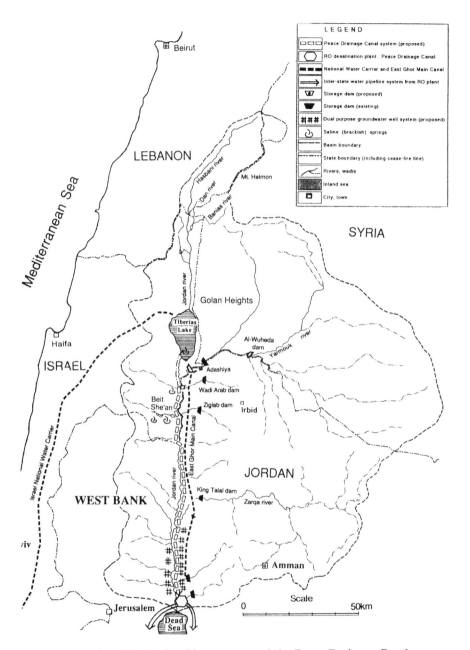

Fig. 11.4 **The Jordan River system and the Peace Drainage Canal**

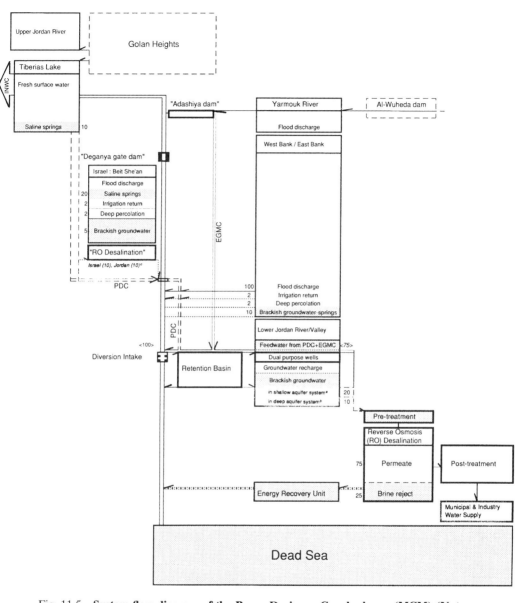

Fig. 11.5 **System flow diagram of the Peace Drainage Canal scheme (MCM) (Notes: PDC = Peace Drainage Canal, EGMC = East Ghor Main Canal, INWC = Israel National Water Carrier;** *a.* **brackish groundwater in shallow aquifer – summer period;** *b.* **brackish groundwater in deep aquifer – drought period;** *c.* **allocation of RO permeate in "Treaty of Peace," October 1994. Source: plans in "Treaty of Peace," October 1994, including Adashiya dam, Deganya Gate dam, and RO desalination plant in Israel)**

165

and the East Bank. The canal route would run alongside the lower Jordan mainstream in either the West Bank or the East Bank. The reverse osmosis desalination plant, including a pre-treatment and post-treatment unit, would be installed at the end of the canal system.

5. *Water pipeline system.* A main waterpipe along the coast of the Dead Sea, to link the major towns of Suwayma, Qumran, Ein Gedi, Ein Bokek, and Al-Mazra'a, would be constructed to share the fresh potable water from the reverse osmosis plant among the three riparian states.

6. *Wastewater treatment system and re-use.* Wastewater treatment facilities in the major towns would be incorporated not only to re-use treated waste water for tree crops or garden irrigation but also to protect the clean water environment of the Dead Sea.

Reverse osmosis desalination

The heart of the Peace Drainage Canal project is the reverse osmosis desalination plant to salvage brackish water. The treatment process includes three phases: pre-treatment, processing, and post-treatment.

Pre-treatment
Before being desalted, the water will pass through three pre-treatment steps to remove all solids that would quickly clog the expensive desalting membranes if they were not removed. Pre-treating the water will ensure a membrane life of three to five years. As the water flows into the plant, chlorine will be added to prevent the growth of algae and other organisms. The water will then go through a grit sedimentation basin to remove heavy grit, sediment, and suspended sands in the water. The water will also be softened by removing some of the calcium. Lime and ferric sulphate are both used in solid contact reactors. In the last step in the pre-treatment process, dual-media filters will be used to remove any fine particles or organisms remaining in the water.

Processing
Reverse osmosis is the separation of one component of a solution from another (in this case, salt from water) by means of pressure exerted on a semi-impermeable plastic membrane. A total of about 6,750 membrane elements inserted into fibreglass pressure vessels will desalt the water. Although the pressure tubes will all be 6 m

(20 ft) in length, some membranes will have a diameter of 30 cm (12 in.), while the diameter of others will be 20 cm (8 in.). The element will be made up of a number of sheets rolled into a spiral-wound membrane. The separation of salt is a chemical process as well as a physical diffusion process. The water will be forced through the walls of cellulose acetate or synthesized membranes by applying pressure at about 15–25 kg/cm^2, allowing only the freshly desalted water to pass through. This process will filtrate 75 per cent of the feed water and remove about 97 per cent of the salts from it. The fresh water will be forced by the downward pressure toward the centre tube.

Post-treatment and energy recovery
The water, with a salinity level of 300–500 mg per litre of TDS, will then be treated to make it safe for drinking in accordance with WHO standards. The water pressure in the brine reject (25 per cent of the feed water with 10,000 mg/litre salinity) will be used to generate electricity with a 1 MW mini hydropower plant at the end of the reverse osmosis module circuit. After retrieving energy of 6.4 million kWh per year, the brine will be directly released to the Dead Sea, where it will mix with this extremely saline water body (300,000 mg/litre of TDS).

Project costs and the unit water cost

The unit cost of the brackish-water reverse osmosis desalination, including the construction of an 85 km drainage canal, is roughly estimated to be US$0.48/m^3. This includes the following four cost elements, assuming a construction period of three years for the reverse osmosis plant and an interest rate of 8 per cent:
– capital cost: US$211,518,000
– design and construction management: US$52,911,000
– financial expenditure: US$68,672,000
– annual operation and maintenance costs: US$20,551,000
The operation and maintenance costs of reverse osmosis desalination would likely be reduced by using less expensive off-peak electricity and by developing low-pressure, high-efficiency membrane modules.

The 75 MCM/yr of water produced from the reverse osmosis plant could be shared equitably among Israel, Palestine, and Jordan (see table 11.1). This water would be mainly used for municipal and industrial water supplies, with the aim of supplying fresh potable water exclusively to the major towns and cities along the shore of the

Table 11.1 **Inter-state water allocation plans for the Jordan River system (MCM per year)**

Proposed plan	Lebanon	Syria	Jordan	Palestine	Israel	Egypt	Total	Remarks
Main Plan (1953)		45	774		394		1,213	
Arab Plan (1954)	35	132	698		182		1,047	
Cotton Plan (1954)	451	30	575		1,290		2,346	including Litani diversion to Jordan
Johnston Plan (1955)								
Hasbani River	35						35	
Banias River		20					20	
Jordan mainstream		22	100		375		497	Israel uses mainstream after Arab states use it
Yarmouk River		90	377		25		492	
East Bank wadis			243				243	
Total	35	132	720		400		1,287	
Treaty of Peace (October 1994)								
Yarmouk River (Adashiya)			25		45		70	Israel: 13 in summer, 33 in winter; Jordan: remainder
Jordan River (Deganya gate)			20		excess		50	Jordan: 20 in summer
RO desalination of saline springs in Israel			10		10		20	
Integrated Joint Plan: Jordan–Palestine–Israel–(Egypt): M. Murakami[a]								
Aqaba hybrid pumped-storage[b]								
Water			34	34	33	33	100	
Hydroelectricity (million kWh/yr)			500		500	500		1.5 billion kWh of electricity is shared by the three
MDS canal for co-generation[c]								
Water			33	34	33		100	
Hydroelectricity (million kWh/yr)			400	400	400			1.2 billion kWh is shared by the riparians with Gaza
Peace Drainage Canal with RO desalination			25	25	25		75	Brackish water desalination by RO

a. Simply assumes an equal allocation of water and electricity. b. Aqaba pumped-storage facilities with hydro-powered desalination plant are situated in the Hashemite Kingdom of Jordan. c. The MDS canal has an intake in Gaza, a conduit in Gaza and Israel, a hydropower station with RO plant in Israel, and a hydro–solar reservoir (Dead Sea) in Jordan, Palestine, and Israel.

Dead Sea. The Peace Drainage Canal scheme with a reverse osmosis desalination plant and water pipeline system should have the highest priority in a basin-wide master plan for an environmentally sound sustainable water development project to foster peaceful cooperation and regional economic development.

The Aqaba hybrid scheme

Construction of any new thermal or nuclear power station in the region would benefit from a pumped-storage scheme for efficient off-peak energy use. Hybrid water–energy co-generation is the application of sea-water pumped-storage with reverse osmosis desalination (Murakami, 1993; Murakami and Musiake, 1994). The Aqaba scheme (see fig. 11.6) would pump sea water during off-peak periods

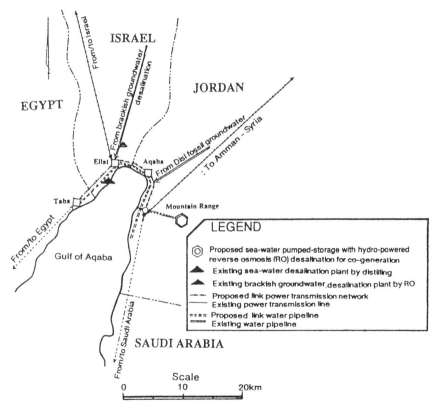

Fig. 11.6 **Aqaba regional development plan with hybrid sea-water pumped-storage scheme for co-generation**

169

to store it in an upper reservoir at the top of an escarpment 600 m above sealevel. The stored sea water would be discharged into a penstock shaft to yield an effective water pressure of 60 kg/cm^2 at the end of the pressure pipe system, simultaneously generating 600 MW of peak electricity and producing 100 MCM of fresh potable water (see fig. 11.7). Off-peak electricity to lift the sea water to 600 m above sealevel would be supplied not only from a steam power plant at Aqaba but also from steam power plants in either Egypt or Israel, or from other regional electricity grids.

Conceptual design

The volume of sea water pumped for co-generation is estimated to be 50 m^3/s, comprising 39 m^3/sec. for peak power electricity generation and 11 m^3/sec. of feed water for reverse osmosis desalination. The theoretical hydro potential to exploit the head difference of 600 m with 39 m^3/sec. of pumped sea water is estimated to be 200 MW, assuming a specific weight of sea water of 1.03 and a synthesized efficiency of 0.85. The discharge and installed capacity of the hydropower plant are preliminarily estimated to be 116 m^3/sec. and 600 MW, respectively, assuming 8 hours a day of marginal peak operation. The annual power output from the 600 MW plant would amount to 1.5 billion kWh with a generating efficiency of 0.85.

Marginal operation of the reverse osmosis system would make use of the hydro-potential energy in a penstock pipeline with 600 m of head difference for 16–24 hours a day. The feed sea-water requirements for producing 100 MCM of permeate per year (with 500–1,000 mg/litre of TDS) are estimated to be 333 MCM, assuming a 30 per cent recovery ratio (70 per cent for brine reject water with 53,000 mg/litre of TDS). The installed capacity of the reverse osmosis unit is estimated to be 322,300 m^3/d with a load factor of 85 per cent.

The potential energy recovery from the brine reject is estimated to be 29.5 MW, assuming 20 per cent of friction loss in the reverse osmosis circuit. The annual production of electricity from the reverse osmosis brine reject is estimated to be 175 million kWh with a load factor of 68 per cent. The brine would then be discharged into the Dead Sea (Murakami and Musiake, 1994). The recovered energy would be used to supply electricity for the post-treatment process or to other pumps to save electricity on the national grid.

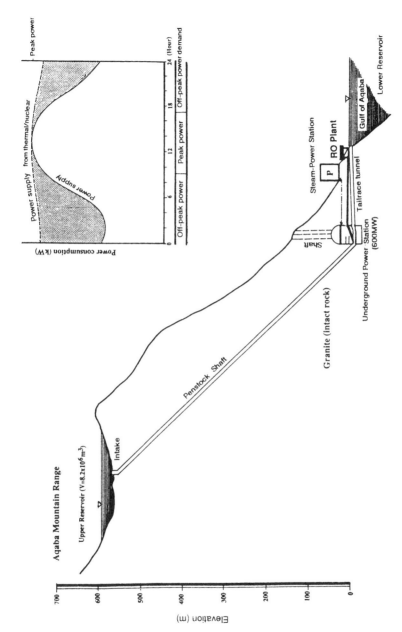

Fig. 11.7 **Schematic profile of the Aqaba hybrid sea-water pumped-storage scheme with reverse osmosis desalination**

171

Table 11.2 **The major cost elements of the Aqaba hybrid sea-water RO desalination unit (preliminary estimates in 1990 prices)**

Major capital cost element (US$)	
Pre-treatment	44,195,000
Desalting plant	70,414,000
RO membrane/equipment	84,835,000
Control and operating system	5,952,000
Appurtenant works	27,013,000
Powerline and substation	11,427,000
Energy recovery/turbine[a]	2,999,000
Sub-total	246,835,000
Design and construction management	62,250,000
Financial expenditure	80,270,000
Total	389,355,000
Major O&M cost element (US$/yr)	
Labour	3,718,000
Material supply	1,860,000
Chemicals	7,440,000
Power (pumped-storage for RO feedwater/permeate[b])	3,100,000
Membrane replacement	28,269,000
Total	44,387,000

a. Energy recovery unit generates electricity from brine reject water of 233 MCM.
b. Assuming US$0.02/kWh of off-peak electricity tariff for pumping 100 MCM.

Cost estimates and water economy

The cost of a unilateral 600 MW pumped-storage scheme is estimated to be US$1 billion at 1990 prices. The total investment cost of the proposed hydro-powered sea-water reverse osmosis desalination plant is preliminarily estimated to be US$389.4 million assuming: a plant life of 20 years, a membrane life (replacement) of 3 years, 8 per cent interest during the three years of construction, the exclusion of cost benefits from energy recovery, and the exclusion of the costs of source water and pipeline/distribution (Murakami, 1991, 1993). The annual costs are estimated to be US$18.6 million in financing the major capital cost element and US$44.4 million in operation and maintenance (O&M) elements, as shown in table 11.2.

Water economy is examined by comparing the unilateral pumped-storage scheme and the hybrid pumped-storage scheme with reverse osmosis desalination. The annual benefit of the hybrid scheme is 1.4 times greater than the unilateral scheme, assuming tariffs of US$0.1/

kWh of peak electricity and US$1.0/m^3 of fresh potable water. The cost and benefit elements are shown in table 11.3.

The unit water cost of hydro-powered sea-water reverse osmosis desalination, which assumes a *shadow benefit* of using 11 m^3/sec. of feed water for the sole purpose of hydroelectricity generation, is estimated to be US$0.69/m^3 $(=0.63 + 0.059)$. The economy of this method can be seen when it is compared with either US$1.6–2.7/m^3 for conventional desalination such as reverse osmosis and multi-stage flush (Murakami 1991, 1995) or unilateral hydropower (see table 11.3).

Method of sharing resources and benefits

The Aqaba hybrid sea-water pumped-storage scheme for co-generation would include the following inter-state cooperation scenarios to share the resources and benefits:

1. An inter-state electricity grid or network that would include Egypt, Israel, Palestine, Jordan, and Saudi Arabia is incorporated in the plan to transfer inexpensive night and morning off-peak electricity to the pumped-storage scheme (buying) and to deliver valuable day and evening peak electricity to neighbouring states (selling).

2. An inter-state water pipeline system connecting three states (Egypt, Israel, and Jordan) along the Aqaba coastline is constructed in order to share fresh potable water from the hydro-powered reverse osmosis desalination plant at Aqaba, Jordan.

3. An inter-state sanitation and water environment management programme, which includes treated wastewater recovery for tree crop and garden irrigation as well as for protecting the clean water environment of Aqaba bay, will be incorporated in the plan. The application of membrane separation technology, including micro-filter and/or ultra-filter techniques, will also be adopted in the process of tertiary wastewater treatment for re-use for limited irrigation (Murakami and Musiake 1994; Murakami, 1995).

Fresh potable water amounting to 100 MCM per year from the Aqaba hydro-powered reverse osmosis desalination plant in the pumped-storage scheme could be shared among Jordan (Aqaba), Israel (Eilat), Egypt (Taba), and Saudi Arabia (Haq) in accordance with a possible agreement within the inter-state regional economic development programme (see fig. 11.6). The non-oil-producing state of Jordan, whose national economy is not as strong as those of Israel and Saudi Arabia, would have an exclusive chance to export 100

Table 11.3 **Cost and benefit elements between unilateral and co-generation schemes (assuming tariffs of US$0.1/kWh of peak electricity and US$1.0/m³ of potable fresh water)**

Type	Feed water (MMC/sec)	Electricity (million kWh/yr)	Permeate (MMC/yr)	Output/Sale[a] (US$m./yr)	Project cost (US$m.)	Annual cost element (US$m.)			
						Capital	O&M	Total	Difference[b]
Unilateral pumped-storage (for power generation only):									
Hydroelectricity	50	1,482		148.2	1,000	50.0	10.0	60.0	88.2
Hybrid pumped-storage with hydro-powered RO desalination:									
Hydroelectricity	39	1,156		139.6	905	39.0	10.0	49.0	
RO desalination	11	175	100	100.0[a]	390	18.6	44.4	63.0	
Total	50	1,331	100	239.6	1,295	57.6	54.4	112.0	127.6

a. Output/Sale does not include the benefit of energy recovery of 175 million kWh in the RO unit.
b. Difference = (Annual output/sale – Annual cost in total).

MCM per year of fresh, potable water. It would also be able to export valuable peak electricity as well as to import cheap off-peak electricity from Israel, Egypt, and Saudi Arabia. The Aqaba hydro-powered sea-water desalination plant would also save 17.5 MCM of fossil groundwater currently being pumped from the Disi aquifer to Aqaba for its municipal water supply (Murakami and Musiake, 1991).

Inter-state cooperation for joint development and use among the riparian parties (including Jordan, Israel, Egypt, and Saudi Arabia) takes into account the following: efficient use and/or saving of energy or oil, with an initiative for global environment perspectives; a long-term flexible supply of peak electricity and fresh water; and fewer political constraints, with geo-political initiatives, incentives, and favours for Jordan. The pumped-storage facility would pump water up to a higher elevation for storage during off-peak hours and would simultaneously produce fresh water and hydroelectricity whenever demand peaked. This facility would be conceived for initial incorporation into the canal project. The hybrid sea-water pumped-storage scheme for co-generation is at the planning stage, but it will be important to spell out the coordination required, including international cooperation, in the next phase of projects that will also need innovative research including membrane separation technologies.

Techno-political assessment of the Peace Drainage Canal and the Med/Red–Dead Sea canal

The water budget of the Dead Sea indicates that a decrease of inflow from the Jordan River catchment would result in the additional introduction of Mediterranean water, thereby increasing the system's hydro-potential energy. Without the Med/Red–Dead Sea Canal project, the Dead Sea will continue to drop in level and shrink in size (see table 11.4). Although not much wildlife is being affected (except for bacteria, the Dead Sea is appropriately named), potash works and health resorts on both shores will continue to contend with the costs of an increasingly distant shoreline. One clear environmental benefit of the project would be the restoration of the Dead Sea to its historical level.

The Declaration of Principles between Israel and the PLO on 13 September 1993 would suggest that the best priority project is to connect the Mediterranean Sea (Gaza) and the Dead Sea by a series of canals and a tunnel conduit with a total length of 100 km. The original idea of the Med–Dead Sea (MDS) Canal scheme was con-

Table 11.4 Approximate water budget of the Dead Sea with non-conventional techno-political alternative schemes (MCM/yr)

	Before 1948	After 1967	Plus MDS	Plus MDS + PDC
Ground elevation below sealevel (m)	−391[a]	−406	−391	−392
Surface area of the Dead Sea (km^2)	1,000	900	1,000	1,000
Annual flow potential from the whole catchment	1,600	1,600	1,600	1,600
Inflow from catchment of the Jordan River	1,100	400	224[b]	211[b]
Inflow from catchment of the Dead Sea	500	400	223[b]	211[b]
Abstraction of flow from the whole catchment	nil	800	1,153[b]	1,178[b]
Evaporation from the Dead Sea surface	−1,600	−1,500		
Evaporation after impounding sea water from Mediterranean			−1,900	−1,900
Tailrace water from MDS hydropower station			1,220	1,220
Brine reject water from RO plant in MDS			233	233
Brine reject water from RO plant in PDC				25
Inflow potential from the whole catchment	1,600	800	447[b]	422[b]
Flow balance	0	−700	0	0

a. The historical equilibrium water level of the Dead Sea before 1930–1948 had been −391m. It will take several decades to fill up the Dead Sea to its historical equilibrium level with sea water at 1,600–2,000 MCM.
b. Some residual flows from the catchment that could be developed at future stages.

ceived in a feasibility study by Israel in 1980 to elaborate the best alternative of 27 optional routes (WPDC, 1980). The trilateral economic committee (Jordan, Israel, and the World Bank) on the integrated development of the Jordan Valley elaborated some new ideas on the Red–Dead Sea Canal in 1994 (World Bank, 1994). Their canal route has a length of 200 km. The original idea was examined by Jordan in 1981 (JVA, 1981; WPDC, 1983). Either of these two strategic options would be a confidence-building measure in the Dead Sea region to supply peak hydroelectricity with or without a supply of fresh potable water by hydro-powered reverse osmosis desalination (Murakami, 1991, 1995; WPDC, 1989).

The reverse osmosis desalination in the Peace Drainage Canal scheme would also substantially reduce discharges into the Dead Sea. This could add 10 MW of hydro potential (60 million kWh per year of electricity) if the Med–Dead Canal or the Red–Dead Canal is incorporated in the integrated development plan.

A techno-political assessment of non-conventional strategic alternatives, comparing the implications of the "Treaty of Peace" before and after 26 October 1994, is shown in table 11.5 (Wolf and Murakami, 1994). The priority projects of the Peace Drainage Canal, the Aqaba hybrid sea-water pumped-storage scheme, and the MDS Canal for co-generation should be integrated into a strategic master plan for the development of the Jordan Rift Valley.

Conclusion

Inter-state regional economic development is considered to be a key element in sustaining the peace process in the region. The Peace Drainage Canal scheme should have the highest priority in the next phase of an international cooperation programme. This environmentally sound, non-conventional water development and management scheme not only takes into account the incentives for eco-political decision-making but also introduces the opportunity for inter-state regional economic development by adding fresh potable water of 75 MMC at a cost of US$0.48/m^3.

In a broader context, Aqaba regional development using hybrid sea-water pumped storage for co-generation is possibly of even greater importance for economic development in the whole region because it includes initiatives, incentives, and favours for Jordan. Hydro-powered sea-water desalination in the hybrid pumped-storage system would simultaneously conserve fossil groundwater in Disi.

Table 11.5 Techno-political assessment for the Dead Sea and Aqaba schemes before and after the "Treaty of Peace" between Jordan and Israel of 26 October 1994

Techno-political alternatives	Technical feasibility				Environmental feasibility	Economic feasibility			Political feasibility	Overall feasibility
	Quantity	Quality	Reliability	Sub-total		Financial viability	Benefit/cost	Sub-total		
Weight (%)	12.5	5.0	7.5	25.0	25.0	12.5	12.5	25.0	25.0	100.0
After the "Treaty of Peace"										
Lower Jordan River Peace Drainage Canal with RO desalination	31.0	66.0	62.0	47.3	55.8	61.0	61.0	61.0	69.0	58.3
Aqaba pumped-storage scheme with hydro-powered sea-water RO desalination	32.5	68.8	57.5	47.3	45.0	52.9	53.6	53.3	53.0	49.6
MDS hydro–solar development with hydro-powered sea-water RO desalination	40.0	72.5	60.0	52.5	45.0	33.8	48.3	41.1	35.3	43.5
Dead Sea pumped-storage	15.0	30.0	60.0	31.5	40.0	53.3	40.0	46.7	46.7	41.2
Mediterranean–Dead Sea Canal, without RO desalination	23.8	31.3	61.3	36.6	22.5	36.3	30.0	33.2	38.5	32.7
Red–Dead Sea Canal, without RO desalination	21.3	30.0	28.8	25.3	22.5	33.8	30.0	31.9	44.2	31.0
Before the "Treaty of Peace"										
Lower Jordan River Peace Drainage Canal with RO desalination	31.0	66.0	62.0	47.3	55.8	61.0	61.0	61.0	69.0	58.3
Aqaba pumped-storage scheme with hydro-powered sea-water RO desalination	32.5	68.8	57.5	47.3	26.3	37.0	37.5	37.3	24.0	33.7
MDS hydro–solar development with hydro-powered sea-water RO desalination	40.0	72.5	60.0	52.5	45.0	33.8	33.8	33.8	35.3	41.7
Dead Sea pumped-storage	15.0	30.0	60.0	31.5	40.0	53.3	40.0	46.7	46.7	41.2
Mediterranean–Dead Sea Canal, without RO desalination	23.8	31.3	61.3	36.6	22.5	36.3	30.0	33.2	38.5	32.7
Red–Dead Sea Canal, without RO desalination	21.3	30.0	28.8	25.3	22.5	33.8	30.0	31.9	31.0	27.7

Sources: before the "Treaty of Peace" – Wolf and Murakami (1994, Ref. 13); after the "Treaty of Peace" – some details on cost estimates and environment impact analysis were added by Murakami.

178

The unit water cost of hydro-powered reverse osmosis desalination is preliminarily estimated to be US$0.69/m³. Such a scheme would be even more competitive when compared with a single-purpose hydro-power scheme such as Dead Sea pumped storage or Med/Red–Dead Sea Canal for power generation only. The new idea of a hybrid sea-water pumped-storage scheme for co-generation at Aqaba will be carefully examined to compare its feasibility and benefits in relation to the other strategic options, including the Med/Red–Dead Canal.

The proposed co-generation schemes would have a flexible capacity to reallocate outputs and benefits in response to a long-term change in demand for water and peak electricity, thus introducing some in-centives for peaceful cooperation and inter-state regional economic development. Once a canal system and reverse osmosis desalination plant were in place, even under different sovereignties, the incentive to connect two or three more states, later, in order to develop consequent ancillary projects could be powerful enough to induce ever-increasing cooperation. The riparians of the Dead Sea and Aqaba bay, including Israel, Palestine (West Bank), and Jordan (East Bank), would see the possibility of achieving comprehensive economic development and a lasting peace to share the region's resources and benefits.

Acknowledgements

I wish to express my deep appreciation to Prof. Katsumi Musiake of the University of Tokyo and Prof. Yuzo Akatsuka of Saitama University. Special thanks are due to Profs. Asit K. Biswas (chairman of the International Water Resources Association Committee on International Waters), John Kolars (University of Michigan), John Waterby (Princeton University), and Aaron T. Wolf (University of Alabama) for their guidance and invaluable advice. I am also grateful to Prof. Heitor Gurgulino De Souza and Dr. Juha Uitto of the United Nations University, who managed the strategic research project on water for peace and conflict resolution of the interna-tional waters in the Middle East, and to the staff of the World Bank, including Mr. Usaid El-Hambali, Mr. John S. Ijichi, Mr. Yo Kimura, Mr. John A. Hayward, Dr. Ulrich Kuffner, and Mr. Alexander MacPhail, for their comments and information.

References

Glueckstern, P. 1982. "Preliminary consideration of combining a large reverse osmosis plant with the Mediterranean–Dead Sea project." *Desalination* 40, pp. 143–156.

JVA (Jordan Valley Authority). 1981 "Potential for the development of hydropower between the Red Sea and Dead Sea." Harza Overseas Engineering Co., Ltd., Main Report.

Murakami, M. 1991. "Arid zone water resources planning study with applications of non-conventional alternatives." Ph.D thesis, University of Tokyo, Japan, December.

—— 1993. "Hydro-powered reverse osmosis (RO) desalination for co-generation: A Middle East case study." *Proceedings of the IDA and WRPC World Congress on Desalination and Water Treatment: Vol. II.* Yokohama, Japan, pp. 37–44.

—— 1995. *Managing Water for Peace in the Middle East: Alternative Strategies.* Tokyo: United Nations University Press.

Murakami, M. and K. Musiake. 1991. "Hydro-powered reverse osmosis (RO) desalination for co-generation." *Proceedings of IWRA International Seminar on "Efficient Water Use"*, Mexico City, pp. 688–695.

—— 1994. "Non-conventional water resources development alternatives to satisfy the water demand of 21st century." *Proceedings of XIII IWRA World Congress on Water Resources*, October, Cairo, Egypt. International Water Resources Association, vol. 1, pp. (T5–S1)2.1–19.

Tahal Israel. 1982. *Dead Sea Power Station: Interim Report on Present State of Planning.* Report prepared for the Mediterranean–Dead Sea Co.

Wolf, A. T. and M. Murakami. 1994. "Techno-political decision making for water resources development: The Jordan River watershed." *Proceedings of XIII IWRA World Congress on Water Resources*, October, Cairo, Egypt. International Water Resources Association, vol. 2, pp. (T5–S2)7.1–16.

World Bank. 1994. "Integrated Development of the Jordan Rift Valley." Draft, October, pp. 6–19.

WPDC (Water Power and Dam Construction). 1980. "Israel decides on canal route." *International News*, October, p. 4.

—— 1983. "Jordan attacks Dead Sea project." *International News*, March, p. 4.

—— 1989. "Dead Sea P-S scheme revived." *World News*, May, p. 3.

Part V
International organizations and inland seas

12

The role of international organizations in the integrated management of international water bodies: The activities of the UNU, UNEP, and the World Bank in the Middle East

Mikiyasu Nakayama

International water bodies require integrated management

National interests among countries are likely to diverge when it comes to international water bodies. Given the international context, however, inefficiency caused by interdependent water uses cannot be resolved through a single government's policies. Upstream countries tend to see little benefit from increasing or maintaining the flow and quality of water for downstream countries. Without enforceable international water-use rights established by treaty, countries make decisions without considering the consequences for other basin countries. However, securing such international agreements and putting them into practice is often difficult. The end result may be environmental, social, and economic losses in the downstream countries that are greater than the benefits to the upstream countries.

More than 200 river basins are shared by two or more countries. These basins account for about 60 per cent of the earth's land area. Fragmented planning and development of the associated transboundary river, lake, and coastal basins are the rule rather than the exception. Although more than 300 treaties have been signed by countries to deal with specific concerns about international water resources and more than 2,000 treaties have provisions related to water, coordinated management of international river basins is still rare, resulting in economic losses, environmental degradation, and international conflict (World Bank, 1993).

International conferences such as the 1992 Dublin Conference on Water and the Environment and the 1992 UN Conference on Environment and Development (UNCED) in Rio de Janeiro, Brazil, have stressed the need for the comprehensive management of water resources, using the river basin as the focus of analysis. Cooperation and good will among states sharing a drainage basin are essential for the efficient development and utilization of international rivers and groundwater aquifers. In order to fulfil their own economic goals, it is important that such states formally collaborate to exchange data, share water, preserve the environment, and generate development programmes that are of mutual interest and joint benefit (World Bank, 1994a).

The need for international efforts and a role for international organizations

Basin states in developing regions may lack the capacity to develop and manage their own portion of shared water resources. The international community may provide both technical and financial supports to develop and implement an integrated water resources management scheme. Through cooperation, states may obtain aid that might not otherwise be available to them (LeMarquand, 1981).

Overcoming institutional barriers, between riparians and within the various basin countries, to the management of international watercourses is not an easy task. Managing institutions, such as river basin authorities, often involve only one ministry in a basin country, and the decisions of such an institute may not be conveyed to the central decision-making mechanism of that basin country. Thus, specific treaties or agreements are needed to codify the responsibilities of participating nations and the facilitating agency. The lessons of experience with agreements and joint actions between riparians, such as the World Bank's difficult but successful nine-year effort to facilitate the 1960 Indus Water Treaty between India and Pakistan, suggest that external assistance and encouragement are valuable and sometimes essential ingredients in establishing international water agreements. Where the basic institutional framework exists, international agencies should provide support and encouragement. However, in case the regional institutional framework does not work satisfactorily, an international organization could still serve as a mediator. It was actually the case with the Interim Mekong Secretariat, which was composed of three basin countries of the Mekong river basin, in the 1991–1995 period. The member states failed to solve by themselves the "veto power" issue, namely if a riparian country could put a veto on another basin country's project in an international water body, and the United Nations Development Programme (UNDP) acted in a mediatory role to get through the impasse and let the basin countries develop a new agreement (Nakayama, 1997). International agencies can also assist riparians in developing and managing water resources and in facilitating the implementation of treaties.

The three main objectives of international efforts should be (a) to help riparian countries address their problems with international water resources, (b) to remove the obstacles to priority development activities that are usually held hostage by disputes over shared watercourses, and (c) to reduce inefficiencies in the use and development of scarce water resources caused by the lack of cooperative planning and development. Since no single international organization commands all the skills, experience, or resources necessary to achieve the needed cooperation, collaborative efforts among potential donors, international organizations, and non-governmental organizations (NGOs) would promote the sound management of international waters (World Bank, 1993).

The cooperation and good will of riparian countries are essential ingredients for the efficient development and utilization of international waterways. International organizations should attach the utmost importance to riparians entering into appropriate cooperative arrangements for such purposes, and stand ready to assist them in achieving these objectives. In cases where differences remain unsolved, international organizations should require that the country offer to negotiate in good faith with other riparians in order to reach appropriate agreements or arrangements (World Bank, 1994b).

Experience in the past has shown that the use of third parties in a mediator's role can facilitate dispute resolution, guide complex bargaining toward acceptable outcomes, and help maintain balance and commitment by riparian countries to the negotiating process (World

Bank, 1994c). International organizations, such as the United Nations University (UNU), the United Nations Environmental Programme (UNEP), or the World Bank, have many advantages as such a third party because each one of these can (a) act as an independent broker; (b) provide leadership inherent in its international role in donor coordination; (c) catalyse the mobilization of official as well as private funding; (d) provide an important channel for gaining access to expertise; (e) be creative in promoting appropriate process solutions; and (f) help ensure systematic evaluation of alternative solutions through the appropriate use of analytical techniques.

The UNU: Accomplishments to promote sound management of international waters

The UNU is an autonomous academic organization under the United Nations umbrella. Environment and sustainable development form one of its five major areas of concentration. The programme area entitled "Environment" responds to the United Nations' Agenda 21. The overall objectives of UNU activities in the field of management of international waters focus on the comprehensive and objective study of regions that share major international water bodies, with a view to providing bases for the sustainable environmental and political management of critical resources (Uitto, 1995).

The UNU Middle East Water Forum was organized, together with the International Water Resources Association (IWRA) and UNEP, in Cairo in February 1993. Participants invited to the Forum in their private capacities (27 leading authorities on Middle East waters) discussed the complex problems of sharing the limited water resources available in a very arid region (Biswas, 1994; Murakami, 1995; Wolf, 1995). Participants found the Forum useful in terms of developing personal contacts, new ideas, and an improved understanding of many technical facts. As a result of the Forum, the Middle East Water Commission was established.

Another UNU activity relates to environmental management of the Aral Sea region. The Aral Sea has been one of the regions studied under the UNU project on "Critical Zones in Global Environmental Change" (Kasperson et al., 1995). As an international (but not as an intergovernmental) academic institute, the UNU, through its global networks of scholars, has been actively involved in the identification of problems and solutions to water issues in the Middle East and other regions.

Assistance given by UNEP and the World Bank to the Aral Sea programme

The Aral Sea basin covers an area of over 690,000 km², which is shared by Kazakhstan, Kyrgyzstan, Tajikistan, Turkmenistan, and Uzbekistan. Small portions of its headwaters are located in Afghanistan, Iran, and China. The basin contains the two largest rivers of Central Asia – the Amudarya and the Syrdarya. These rivers are fed by the snowmelt and glaciers from the mountains. The Amudarya's sources are mostly located in Tajikistan, with a few watercourses originating in north-eastern Afghanistan. The Syrdarya originates mainly in Kyrgyzstan. It runs across small portions of Tajikistan and Uzbekistan and through the Kazakh provinces of Chimkent and Kzyl-Orda (World Bank, 1994d).

In 1960 the Aral Sea was the fourth-largest inland lake in the world. Since then, however, its area and volume have decreased significantly to sixth place. This resulted from the fact that the river inflows from the Amudarya and Syrdarya have greatly diminished as a direct result of water withdrawals for newly developed irrigated farmlands both within and outside the catchment. By 1989 the sealevel had fallen by 14.3 m and the surface area had shrunk from 68,000 km² to 37,000 km². The salinity of the Sea had increased to eight times its 1960 level. The major environmental problems now observed in the Aral Sea basin include: the reduction of the Sea, the destruction of its aquatic ecosystem, the degradation of soil quality in many parts of the basin, pollution of surface water and groundwater of the delta areas, depressed economic activity owing to the collapse of the Aral fishery and related small industries, and adverse health impacts on the population because of the lack of safe potable water and food.

Inefficient irrigation practices coupled with heavy chemical applications, cultivation of cotton and rice, and inappropriate development policies are among the important causes. The Soviet policy for the region in the 1950s and 1960s called for the expansion of irrigated agriculture in the Amudarya and Syrdarya basins in order to promote cotton production, so that the Soviet Union could become self-sufficient in this commodity. The area devoted to paddy-rice production was also extended, despite the fact that the region is so close to the northernmost agro-climatic limit of rice cultivation. The primitive irrigation techniques applied induced massive leakage and evaporation, which led to the waterlogging and salinization of the irrigated fields.

Recognizing the crucial need to save the disappearing Aral Sea and the need to provide an overall perspective of the Aral region, the former Soviet Union, in 1989, asked UNEP to work on the environmental issues of the Aral Sea basin. UNEP has been working on the environmental management of international river and lake basins within the framework of its EMINWA (Environmentally sound Management of INland WAters) since 1985 (David et al., 1988). The EMINWA programme is designed to encourage and assist governments to integrate environmental considerations into their management and development of inland water resources, with a view to reconciling conflicting interests and ensuring the harmonious regional development of water resources – harmonious with regard to the water-related environment throughout entire water systems. The most important aim of the EMINWA programme is to introduce this synthetic approach to the management and development of freshwater resources on a basinwide scale and to promote sustainable development in entire inland water systems. The first priority is to help countries that share common river/lake/aquifer basins to develop their water resources in a sustainable manner and to use them without conflict. UNEP had assisted basin countries of the Zambezi River basin (David, 1988) and of the Lake Chad basin before it was asked by the former Soviet Union to work on the Aral Sea basin.

As a result of meetings of the working group of experts and field visits, a report ("Diagnostic Study for the Development of an Action Plan for the Aral Sea") was issued by UNEP in September 1992. The objectives of the Diagnostic Study were, within the framework of the EMINWA programme of UNEP, (a) to define specific environmental problems and their impacts in the present and the foreseeable future, and to help basin countries to formulate programmes for the incorporation of environmental concerns into the management of water resources, and (b) to increase the awareness of various governmental institutions involved in socio-economic development activities about their potential impacts within the basin, and to encourage potential donor countries to contribute to the implementation of the projects (David et al., 1988).

The Diagnostic Study presented a comprehensive analysis of the causes of the Aral Sea crisis, but did not recommend a specific action plan. It provided, however, a basis for elaboration and analysis of the strategies for further activities for mitigating the consequences of the ecological disaster. Upon completion of the Diagnostic Study by UNEP, the World Bank took over the role of coordinator of Aral Sea activities among basin countries, donor countries, and international organizations. In response to requests for assistance from the five "Aral Sea republics," a World Bank mission visited the region in late September 1992. After a review of existing reports, field visits, and discussions with the ministries and local officials of the region, the mission presented an *aide-mémoire* recommending four major thrusts to address the Aral crisis: (a) stabilizing the environment of the Sea; (b) rehabilitating the disaster zone around the Sea; (c) undertaking comprehensive management of the international waters; and (d) building regional institutions to plan and implement the above programmes (World Bank, 1994e).

The World Bank, in collaboration with UNEP and the UNDP, organized an international seminar in Washington D.C. in April 1993 to mobilize the support of donor countries and international agencies for the proposed programme to address the crisis. Ministerial-level representatives of the five Aral Sea basin states presented their respective heads of states' message requesting international support for the programme and confirmed their strong commitment to cooperate in order to address the Aral Sea crisis. The donors supported a Central Asian proposal to establish a "Fund" and provided a substantial grant to finance the start of work on the first phase of the programme.

The "Aral Sea Program – Phase 1" was subsequently formulated by the Executive Committee of the newly established Central Asian Republics' Interstate Council for Addressing the Aral Sea Crisis, with assistance from the World Bank, UNEP, and the UNDP. The Program has four main objectives: (a) to stabilize the environment of the Aral Sea Basin; (b) to rehabilitate the disaster zone around the Sea; (c) to improve the management of the international waters of the Aral Sea basin; and (d) to build the capacity of the regional institutions to plan and implement the above programmes. The Phase 1 Program included 19 projects designated to achieve the objectives stated above. In broad terms, 3 projects were intended to initiate the first steps to improve conditions in the disaster zone, 7 projects were intended to improve conditions in the disaster zone, and 9 projects were centred on managing the water resources of the basin. In addition to 19 projects, the Program included a separate project for building the capacity of the regional institutions to plan and implement the Program.

Based on the fact that the basin countries of the Aral Sea (a) agreed upon the Program, and (b) decided to establish a river basin organization, some donor countries have developed their projects along with the Program. This suggests that the assistance given by international organizations has proved quite effective in accomplishing some of these achievements, which might not otherwise have been attained in such a short time-frame.

Programme for the Caspian Sea basin as an international effort

The Caspian Sea is the largest closed basin lake in the world. The Sea is about 1,200 km long and about 310 km wide. Its coastline is approximately 7,000 km long. The area of the Sea is 386,400 km^2, measured at 27.5 m below mean sealevel, and its drainage basin is 3.1 million km^2. Five nations – Azerbaijan, the Islamic Republic of Iran, Kazakhstan, Russia, and Turkmenistan – share the catchment. The Caspian Sea possesses a variety of marine and coastal ecosystems. Several important economic activities in the Caspian have a bearing on the Caspian environment. These include stocks of sturgeon, on which many people in fisheries depend for a livelihood, and which are an important source of export revenue. Oil exploration and exploitation around the Caspian are also of major importance.

The level of the Caspian Sea over the past 100 years has exhibited a clearly expressed tendency towards lowering. In 1977, the level reached a record low mark of 29.0 m below mean sealevel (Rodionov, 1990). As the Sea declined, human activities such as farming shifted onto the newly exposed seabed. The Soviet government responded with engineering solutions, developing plans to bring water to the Sea from wetter parts of the Soviet Union (Glantz, 1995). Shortly after this record low, the water level of the Caspian began to rise. This rise has been unusual in terms of the rate of its acceleration and, more importantly, its uninterrupted duration (Rodionov, 1990). Environmental problems are mounting: coastal inundation because of sealevel rise, water pollution by raw sewage and oil production, fishing pressure and its impacts on fish populations (especially sturgeon, the main source of high-value caviar) (Glantz, 1995). The fall in lake level between 1927 and 1977 resulted in lakeward encroachment of all kinds of economic activity, not the least important of which has been those of the petroleum industry. These included oil exploration, oil field development, and pipeline construction. Shoreline changes necessitated the lakeward movement of facilities such as moorages, docks, embankments, etc., as the lake area decreased. The unexpected rise in the lake's level since 1977 has

190

caused the inundation of everything built on the exposed lakebed during the course of the 50 years of lake-level decline (Shafer, 1994). The Caspian basin countries and their peoples face significant environmental and resource management issues and problems, many of which are interrelated. These issues and problems have not yet been analysed in a comprehensive and systematic manner.

During the past several years, the Caspian Sea coastal states have undertaken a number of initiatives with respect to the environmental protection of the Caspian Sea. In 1991, the basin countries organized the first multilateral conference on the environmental problems of the Caspian Sea, which called for international coordination of activities aimed at the protection of the marine environment and the establishment of an international monitoring system. At Almaty, Kazakhstan, in May 1994, the coastal countries held a regional meeting on the implications of climate change for the Caspian Sea region. In the "Declaration on Environmental Cooperation in the Caspian Sea" adopted by the five basin countries, the provisions of the draft Convention for the Conservation and Utilization of Bioresources of the Caspian Sea were reaffirmed (Meeting of the Representatives of the Caspian Sea, 1994). Concern was expressed about environmental degradation of the Caspian Sea basin, particularly in its coastal zone, and about marine biological resources. The states declared that:

1. Sealevel rise, irrational utilization of natural resources, and other adverse factors represent significant risks to the region of the Caspian Sea.
2. Urgent needs exist to define the status of the Caspian Sea and its bio-resources, including specially protected reserve territories and water bodies.
3. The fastest implementation of coordinated measures on stabilization of the ecological situation will prevent further degradation of the ecosystem of the Caspian Sea and its coastal territories.
4. Coordination of international cooperation in research, management, economic incentives, and harmonization of legislation with the goal of conserving the biodiversity of the Caspian Sea and its coastal zone is the highest priority task of all Caspian states.
5. The Caspian Sea states affirm their desire to cooperate constructively in environmental management and actions aimed at sustainable and ongoing utilization of the biological resources of the Caspian Sea.
6. The Caspian Sea states will cooperate fully in the preparation and implementation of programmes of joint activities on protection

of the environment which should establish the basis for rational utilization of natural resources and identify a priority sphere of activities.

7. The representatives of the Caspian Sea states call on the international community to support their joint efforts and provide assistance in the development of the environmental programme.

The meeting called for coordination among the basin countries and international organizations, and agreed to request that UNEP prepare an action plan on the protection and management of the environment of the Caspian Sea. UNEP, UNDP, and the World Bank have agreed to respond to recent policy commitments made by the governments of the basin countries concerning the Caspian environment by embarking on various steps to assist the governments in the preparation and implementation of a comprehensive and integrated environmental and resource management plan for the Caspian (called the Caspian initiative). The ultimate aim of the Caspian initiative would be to facilitate the integrated management and sustainable development of oceans and seas, including enclosed and semi-enclosed seas, and coastal and marine areas (including exclusive economic zones), and the protection, rational use, and development of their natural resources.

Discussion among basin countries of the Caspian Sea and international organizations is in its very early stages. It is, thus, still not known what sort of activities are to be included in a programme that could be developed for the Caspian Sea. However, if the previous successful case in the Aral Sea basin can be viewed as a precursor, similar steps could be taken toward the development of a Caspian programme. A working group of experts, composed of representatives from basin countries, donor countries, international organizations, and NGOs, should be established. A diagnostic study could then be prepared by the working group, as a baseline for understanding the circumstances of the water body and its catchment. A draft programme or a draft action plan could be developed, based on the findings of a Caspian Sea diagnostic study. At the same time, donors' meetings could be organized to let potential donor countries and organizations know the nature of the issue(s) and possible ways and means for solution(s). The programme developed should be adopted by basin countries as a binding document. Riparian countries should also agree upon the implementation scheme for the adopted programme; this may include the establishment of a river/lake basin organization.

Conclusions

Past experiences accumulated by the UNU, UNEP, and the World Bank have shown that the following aspects are essential in promoting the integrated management of international water bodies: collaboration among international organizations and donor agencies; and the involvement of the central decision-making mechanism.

Collaboration among international organizations and donor agencies

Although the importance of collaboration among various organizations, each with a different mandate, has been stressed, it has not always been realized in the past. For example, UNEP developed, between 1985 and 1987, the "Action Plan for the Environmentally Sound Management of the Common Zambezi River System" (David, 1988). The plenipotentiaries of the Zambezi River basin countries (ministries responsible mostly for water and/or environmental matters) signed the International Agreement on the Action Plan for the Environmentally Sound Management of the Common Zambezi River System in 1987 at Harare, Zimbabwe. The implementation of the Action Plan has nevertheless been very sluggish, because only a few donor agencies showed interest in the implementation of the Action Plan (Balek, 1992). As before, development activities in the Zambezi River basin have been conducted in an uncoordinated manner by riparian countries and donor agencies.

International organizations often stress the importance of coordination among basin countries. However, as a matter of fact, basin countries sharing an international water body usually have such mechanisms as a river basin authority or a lake basin commission for this purpose, and the remaining problem is how to make these institutional arrangements functional. Ironically, what is generally lacking is a mechanism that permits international organizations and donor agencies to coordinate their activities in a particular international basin.

One possible excuse for the lack of such a mechanism is that it is only the recipient country that is in a position to provide this mechanism – neither international organizations nor donor agencies are supposed to collaborate by themselves. However, if donor agencies assume that a basin country (in the developing world) lacks the capacity to manage its own water resources (and they provide it with various forms of aid), it would be very naive to presume that the same country would have the capacity to coordinate projects that would be provided by donor agencies. The lack of coordination may stem from the fact that (a) international organizations and donor agencies are themselves competing to support the "better" projects, (b) few of these organizations are willing to be coordinated by another donor agency, (c) little effort has been given to the establishment of a mechanism for coordination, and (d) neither international organizations nor donor agencies are keen to enhance the capability of the recipient country to coordinate aid operations. Thus, efforts are clearly needed to develop an appropriate mechanism so that development activities in an international basin could be coordinated both among basin countries and among international organizations and donor agencies.

The involvement of the central decision-making mechanism

Another essential factor in promoting integrated management of international water bodies is the involvement of the central decision-making mechanism in each basin country. The success of the World Bank in the Indus Water Treaty in getting the agreement of the riparian countries (though the Treaty did not aim at integrated management of the basin) can be attributed to the fact that the Prime Minister of India and the President of Pakistan were involved in the process and consulted throughout the negotiation process. The impasse in the implementation of the Action Plan for the Zambezi River basin may stem from the fact that (a) only ministries in charge of environment in basin countries, which were responsible for UNEP-related issues, participated in the development of the Action Plan, (b) other ministries working on development projects in the basin had little to do with the Action Plan, and (c) the commitment of the central decision-making mechanism in each basin country was not obtained for implementation of the Action Plan.

Implementation of the "Aral Sea Program," promoted by the World Bank, can be used as a prototype because (a) the Program was supported by the top decision makers of the basin countries, (b) efforts were made to coordinate the activities of other international organizations and donor agencies, and (c) ministries in charge of developing projects in the catchment actively participated in the formulation of the Program.

References

Balek, J. 1992. *The Environment for Sale*. New York: Carlton Press.

Biswas, A. K. (ed.). 1994. *International Waters of the Middle East: From Euphrates–Tigris to Nile*. Bombay: Oxford University Press.

David, L. J. 1988. "Environmentally sound management of the Zambezi River Basin." *International Journal of Water Resources Development* 4(2), pp. 80–102.

David, L. J. et al. 1988. "The environmental management of large international basins." *International Journal of Water Resources Development* 4(2), pp. 103–107.

Glantz, M. H. 1995. "In Central Asia, a sea dies: A sea also rises." *Climate-Related Impacts International Network Newsletter* 10(2), p. 1.

Kasperson, J. X., R. E. Kasperson, and B. L. Turner II. 1995. *Regions at Risk: Comparisons of Threatened Environments*. Tokyo: United Nations University Press.

LeMarquand, D. G. 1981. "International action for international rivers." *Water International* 6, pp. 147–151.

Meeting of the Representatives of the Caspian Sea. 1994. *Declaration on Environmental Cooperation in the Caspian Sea*. Meeting of the Representatives of the Caspian Sea, Almaty, Kazakhstan.

Murakami, M. 1995. *Managing Water for Peace in the Middle East: Alternative Strategies*. Tokyo: United Nations University Press.

Nakayama, M. 1997. "Successes and failures of international organizations in dealing with international waters." *International Journal of Water Resources Development*, in press.

Rodionov, S. N. 1990. "A climatological analysis of the unusual recent rise in the level of the Caspian Sea." *Soviet Geography* 31(4), pp. 265–275.

Shafer, J. M. 1994. Caspian Sea lake-level fluctuation and near-shore oil production." *World Resource Review* 6(1), pp. 112–124.

Uitto, J. I. 1995. "Management of International Waters in the UNU Programme." Opening address at the Forum on Caspian, Aral and Dead Sea Perspectives on Water Environment Management, Tokyo, Japan, 28 March 1995. The UNU, the International Lake Environment Committee Foundation (ILEC), and the UNEP International Environmental Technology Centre (IETC).

Wolf, A.T. 1995. *Hydropolitics along the Jordan River: Scarce Water and Its Impact on the Arab–Israeli Conflict*. Tokyo: United Nations University Press.

World Bank. 1993. *Water Resources Management – A World Bank Policy Paper*. Washington, D.C.: World Bank.

———— 1994a. *A Guide to the Formulation of Water Resources Strategy*. World Bank Technical Paper Number 263. Washington, D.C.: World Bank.

———— 1994b. *International Inland Waters*. World Bank Technical Paper Number 239. Washington, D.C.: World Bank.

———— 1994c. *A Strategy for Managing Water in the Middle East and North Africa*. Washington, D.C.: World Bank.

———— 1994d. *Turkmenistan – World Bank Country Study*. Washington, D.C.: World Bank.

———— 1994e. *Aral Sea Program – Phase I. Briefing paper for the proposed donors' meeting to be held on June 23–24, 1994 in Paris*. Washington, D.C.: World Bank.

Contributors

Michael H. Glantz
Environmental and Societal Impacts Group, National Center for Atmospheric Research, USA

Genady N. Golubev
Faculty of Geography, Moscow State University, Russian Federation

Tatsuo Kira
Scientific Committee of the International Lake Environment Committee (ILEC) Foundation, Kusatsu City, Japan

Bo Kjellén
Chairman, Negotiating Committee for the UN Convention to Combat Desertification

Iwao Kobori
School of Political Science and Economics, Meiji University, Japan

Pirouz Mojtahed-Zadeh
Geopolitics and International Boundaries Research Centre, SOAS, University of London, UK

Masahiro Murakami
Nippon Koei Co., Ltd., Consulting Engineers, Japan

Mikiyasu Nakayama
Faculty of Agriculture, Utsunomiya University, Japan

Toshibumi Sakata
Tokai University Research and Information Centre, Japan

Tsuneo Tsukatani
Kyoto University, Japan

Juha I. Uitto
Academic Officer, The United Nations University, Japan

Aaron T. Wolf
Department of Geography, University of Alabama, USA

Index